THOUSAND OAKS LIBRARY

D0824618

DISCARD

COLLECTION MANAGEMENT

8/09	8 - 2	
4/26/12	4 - 3	11/8/11

THOUSAND OAKS LIBRARY
1401 E. Janss Road
Thousand Oaks, CA 91362

career ideas for teens
in architecture and construction

Diane Lindsey Reeves
with Gail Karlitz and Don Rauf

Ferguson
An imprint of ☑®Facts On File

Career Ideas for Teens in Architecture and Construction

Copyright © 2005 by Bright Futures Press

All rights reserved. No part of this book may be reproduced or utilized in any form or by any means, electronic or mechanical, including photocopying, recording, or by any information storage or retrieval systems, without permission in writing from the publisher. For information contact:

Ferguson
An imprint of Facts On File, Inc.
132 West 31st Street
New York NY 10001

Library of Congress Cataloging-in-Publication Data

Reeves, Diane Lindsey, 1959–
   Career ideas for teens in architecture and construction / Diane Lindsey Reeves with Gail Karlitz and Don Rauf.
    p. cm.
   Includes index.
   ISBN 0-8160-5289-1 (hc: alk. paper)
   1. Construction industry—Vocational guidance—Juvenile literature. 2. Architecture—Vocational guidance—Juvenile literature. I. Karlitz, Gail. II. Rauf, Don. III. Title.
HD9715.A2R425 2004
624'.023—dc22

624.023

2004020030

Ferguson books are available at special discounts when purchased in bulk quantities for businesses, associations, institutions, or sales promotions. Please call our Special Sales Department in New York at (212) 967-8800 or (800) 322-8755.

You can find Ferguson on the World Wide Web at http://www.fergpubco.com

Text design by Joel and Sandy Armstrong
Cover design by Nora Wertz
Illustrations by Matt Wood

Printed in the United States of America

VB PKG 10 9 8 7 6 5 4 3 2

This book is printed on acid-free paper.

contents

acknowledgments

A million thanks to the people who took the time to share their career stories and provide photos for this book:

Candace Cain
Robert Decker
Susan Flashman
Patricia Galloway
Christine Hess
Stacey Hovis
Isaac Panzarella
JP Reuer

And a big thank-you to the contributing writers who helped fill these pages with important and interesting information:

Christy Brownlee
Carli Entin
Samantha Henderson

career ideas for teens

welcome to your future

Q: What's one of the most boring questions adults ask teens?

A: "So . . . what do you want to be when you grow up?"

Well-meaning adults always seem so interested in what you plan to be.

You, on the other hand, are just trying to make it through high school in one piece.

But you may still have a nagging feeling that you really need to find some direction and think about what you want to do with your life.

When it comes to choosing your life's work there's some good news and some bad news. The good news is that, according to the U.S. Bureau of Labor Statistics, you have more than 12,000 different occupations to choose from. With that many options there's got to be something that's just right for you.

Right?

Absolutely.

But . . .

Here comes the bad news.

THERE ARE MORE THAN 12,000 DIFFERENT OCCUPATIONS TO CHOOSE FROM!

How in the world are you ever going to figure out which one is right for you?

We're so glad you asked!

Helping high school students like you make informed choices about their future is what this book (and each of the other titles in the *Career Ideas for Teens* series) is all about. Here you'll encounter 10 tough questions designed to help you answer the biggest one of all: "What in the world am I going to do after I graduate from high school?"

The *Career Ideas for Teens* series enables you to expand your horizons beyond the "doctor, teacher, lawyer" responses common to those new to the career exploration process. The books provide a no-pressure introduction to real jobs that real people do. And they offer a chance to "try on" different career options before committing to a specific college program or career path. Each title in this series is based on one of the 16 career clusters established by the U.S. Department of Education.

And what is a career cluster, you ask? Career clusters are based on a simple and very useful concept. Each cluster consists of all entry-level through professional-level occupations in a broad industry area. All of the jobs and industries in a cluster have many things in common. This organizational structure makes it easier for people like you to get a handle on the big world of work. So instead of rushing headlong into a mind-boggling exploration of the entire universe of career opportunities, you get a chance to tiptoe into smaller, more manageable segments first.

We've used this career cluster concept to organize the *Career Ideas for Teens* series of books. For example, careers related to the arts, communication, and entertainment are organized or "clustered" into the *Career Ideas for Teens in the Arts and Communications* title; a wide variety of health care professions are included in *Career Ideas for Teens in Health Science*; and so on.

Clueless as to what some of these industries are all about? Can't even imagine how something like manufacturing or public administration could possibly relate to you?

No problem.

You're about to find out. Just be prepared to expect the unexpected as you venture out into the world of work. There are some pretty incredible options out there, and some pretty surprising ones too. In fact, it's quite possible that you'll discover that the ideal career for you is one you had never heard of before.

Whatever you do, don't cut yourself short by limiting yourself to just one book in the series. You may find that your initial interests guide you towards the health sciences field—which would, of course, be a good place to start. However, you may discover some new "twists" with a look through the arts and communications book. There you may find a way to blend your medical interests with your exceptional writing and speaking skills by considering becoming a public relations (PR) specialist for a hospital or pharmaceutical company. Or look at the book on education to see about becoming a public health educator or school nurse.

Before you get started, you should know that this book is divided into three sections, each representing an important step toward figuring out what to do with your life.

The first eight titles in the *Career Ideas for Teens* series focus on:

- Architecture and Construction
- Arts and Communications
- Education and Training
- Government and Public Service
- Health Science
- Information Technology
- Law and Public Safety
- Manufacturing

Before You Get Started

Unlike most books, this one is meant to be actively experienced, rather than merely read. Passive perusal won't cut it. Energetic engagement is what it takes to figure out something as important as the rest of your life.

As we've already mentioned, you'll encounter 10 important questions as you work your way through this book. Following each Big Question is an activity designated with a symbol that looks like this:

Every time you see this symbol, you'll know it's time to invest a little energy in your future by getting out your notebook or binder, a pen or pencil, and doing whatever the instructions direct you to do. If this book is your personal property, you can choose to do the activities right in the book. But you still might want to make copies of your finished products to go in a binder so they are all in one place for easy reference.

When you've completed all the activities, you'll have your own personal **Big Question AnswerBook**, a planning guide representing a straightforward and truly effective process you can use throughout your life to make fully informed career decisions.

discover you at work

This first section focuses on a very important subject: You. It poses four Big Questions that are designed specifically to help you "discover you":

- ❓ Big Question #1: **who are you?**
- ❓ Big Question #2: **what are your interests and strengths?**
- ❓ Big Question #3: **what are your work values?**

Then, using an interest assessment tool developed by the U.S. Department of Labor and implemented with your very vivid imagination, you'll picture yourself doing some of the things that people actually do for their jobs. In other words, you'll start "discovering you at work" by answering the following:

- ❓ Big Question #4: **what's your work personality?**

Unfortunately, this first step is often a misstep for many people. Or make that a "missed" step. When you talk with the adults in your life about their career choices, you're likely to find that some of them never even considered the idea of choosing a career based on personal preferences and strengths. You're also likely to learn that if they had it to do over again, this step would definitely play a significant role in the choices they would make.

explore your options

There's more than meets the eye when it comes to finding the best career to pursue. There are also countless ways to blend talent or passion in these areas in some rather unexpected and exciting ways. Get ready to find answers to two more Big Questions as you browse through an entire section of career profiles:

❓ Big Question #5: **do you have the right skills?**
❓ Big Question #6: **are you on the right path?**

experiment with success

At long last you're ready to give this thing called career planning a trial run. Here's where you'll encounter three Big Questions that will unleash critical decision-making strategies and skills that will serve you well throughout a lifetime of career success.

While you're at it, take some time to sit in on a roundtable discussion with successful professionals representing a very impressive array of careers related to this industry. Many of their experiences will apply to your own life, even if you don't plan to pursue the same careers.

❓ Big Question #7: **who knows what you need to know?**
❓ Big Question #8: **how can you find out what a career is really like?**
❓ Big Question #9: **how do you know when you've made the right choice?**

Then as you begin to pull all your new insights and ideas together, you'll come to one final question:

❓ Big Question #10: **what's next?**

As you get ready to take the plunge, remember that this is a book about possibilities and potential. You can use it to make the most of your future work!

Here's what you'll need to complete the Big Question AnswerBook:

- A notebook or binder for the completed activities included in all three sections of the book
- An openness to new ideas
- Complete and completely candid answers to the 10 Big Question activities

So don't just read it, do it.
Plan it.
Dream it.

SECTION 1
discover you at work

The goal here is to get some clues about who you are and what you should do with your life. As time goes by, you will grow older, become more educated, and have more experiences, but many things that truly define you are not likely to change. Even now you possess very strong characteristics —genuine qualities that mark you as the unique and gifted person that you undoubtedly are.

It's impossible to overestimate the importance of giving your wholehearted attention to this step. You, after all, are the most valuable commodity you'll ever have to offer a future employer. Finding work that makes the most of your assets often means the difference between enjoying a rewarding career and simply earning a paycheck.

You've probably already experienced the satisfaction of a good day's work. You know what we mean—those days when you get all your assignments in on time, you're prepared for the pop quiz your teacher sprung on you, and you beat your best time during sports practice. You may be exhausted at the end of the day but you can't help but feel good about yourself and your accomplishments. A well-chosen career can provide that same sense of satisfaction. Since you're likely to spend upwards of 40 years doing some kind of work, well-informed choices make a lot of sense!

Let's take a little time for you to understand yourself and connect what you discover about yourself to the world of work.

To find a career path that's right for you, we'll tackle these three Big Questions first:

- **who are you?**
- **what are your interests and strengths?**
- **what are your work values?**

?Big Question #1:
who are you?

Have you ever noticed how quickly new students in your school or new families in your community find the people who are most like them? If you've ever been the "new" person yourself, you've probably spent your first few days sizing up the general population and then getting in with the people who dress in clothes a lot like yours, appreciate the same style of music, or maybe even root for the same sports teams.

Given that this process happens so naturally—if not necessarily on purpose—it should come as no surprise that many people lean toward jobs that surround them with people most like them. When people with common interests, common values, and complementary talents come together in the workplace, the results can be quite remarkable.

Many career aptitude tests, including the one developed by the U.S. Department of Labor and included later in this book, are based on the theory that certain types of people do better at certain types of jobs. It's like a really sophisticated matchmaking service. Take your basic strengths and interests and match them to the strengths and interests required by specific occupations.

It makes sense when you think about it. When you want to find a career that's ideally suited for you, find out what people like you are doing and head off in that direction!

There's just one little catch.

The only way to recognize other people like you is to recognize yourself. Who are you anyway? What are you like? What's your basic approach to life and work?

Now's as good a time as any to find out. Let's start by looking at who you are in a systematic way. This process will ultimately help you understand how to identify personally appropriate career options.

Big Activity #1:
who are you?

On a sheet of paper, if this book doesn't belong to you, create a list of adjectives that best describe you. You should be able to come up with at least 15 qualities that apply to you. There's no need to make judgments about whether these qualities are good or bad. They just are. They represent who you are and can help you understand what you bring to the workforce.

(If you get stuck, ask a trusted friend or adult to help describe especially strong traits they see in you.)

Some of the types of qualities you may choose to include are:

- **How you relate to others:**
  Are you shy? Outgoing? Helpful? Dependent? Empathic? In charge? Agreeable? Challenging? Persuasive? Popular? Impatient? A loner?
- **How you approach new situations:**
  Are you adventurous? Traditional? Cautious? Enthusiastic? Curious?
- **How you feel about change—planned or unplanned:**
  Are you resistant? Adaptable? Flexible? Predictable?
- **How you approach problems:**
  Are you persistent? Spontaneous? Methodical? Creative?
- **How you make decisions:**
  Are you intuitive? Logical? Emotional? Practical? Systematic? Analytical?
- **How you approach life:**
  Are you laid back? Ambitious? Perfectionist? Idealistic? Optimistic? Pessimistic? Self-sufficient?

Feel free to use any of these words if they happen to describe you well, but please don't limit yourself to this list. Pick the best adjectives that paint an accurate picture of the real you. Get more ideas from a dictionary or thesaurus if you'd like.

When you're finished, put the completed list in your Big Question AnswerBook.

Big Activity #1: **who are you?**

fifteen qualities that describe me		
1	2	3
4	5	6
7	8	9
10	11	12
13	14	15
etc.		

Big Question #2:
what are your interests and strengths?

For many people, doing something they like to do is the most important part of deciding on a career path—even more important than how much money they can earn!

We don't all like to do the same things—and that's good. For some people, the ideal vacation is lying on a beach, doing absolutely nothing; others would love to spend weeks visiting museums and historic places. Some people wish they had time to learn to skydive or fly a plane; others like to learn to cook gourmet meals or do advanced math.

If we all liked the same things, the world just wouldn't work very well. There would be incredible crowds in some places and ghost towns in others. Some of our natural resources would be overburdened; others would never be used. We would all want to eat at the same restaurant, wear the same outfit, see the same movie, and live in the same place. How boring!

So let's get down to figuring out what you most like to do and how you can spend your working life doing just that. In some ways your answer to this question is all you really need to know about choosing a career, because the people who enjoy their work the most are those who do something they enjoy. We're not talking rocket science here. Just plain old common sense.

Big Activity # 2:

what are your interests and strengths?

Imagine this: No school, no job, no homework, no chores, no obligations at all. All the time in the world you want to do all the things you like most. You know what we're talking about—those things that completely grab your interest and keep you engrossed for hours without your getting bored. Those kinds of things you do really well—sometimes effortlessly, sometimes with extraordinary (and practiced) skill.

And, by the way, EVERYONE has plenty of both interests and strengths. Some are just more visible than others.

Step 1: Write the three things you most enjoy doing on a sheet of paper, if this book doesn't belong to you. Leave lots of space after each thing.

Step 2: Think about some of the deeper reasons why you enjoy each of these activities—the motivations beyond "it's fun." Do you enjoy shopping because it gives you a chance to be with your friends? Because it allows you to find new ways to express your individuality? Because you enjoy the challenge of finding bargains or things no one else has discovered? Or because it's fun to imagine the lifestyle you'll be able to lead when you're finally rich and famous? In the blank spaces, record the reasons why you enjoy each activity.

Step 3: Keep this list handy in your Big Question AnswerBook so that you can refer to it any time you have to make a vocational decision. Sure, you may have to update the list from time to time as your interests change. But one thing is certain. The kind of work you'll most enjoy will be linked in some way to the activities on that list. Count on it.

Maybe one of your favorite things to do is "play basketball." Does that mean the only way you'll ever be happy at work is to play professional basketball?

Maybe.

Maybe not.

Use your *why* responses to read between the lines. The *whys* can prove even more important than the *whats*. Perhaps what you like most about playing basketball is the challenge or the chance to be part of a team that shares a common goal. Maybe you really like pushing yourself to improve. Or it could be the rush associated with competition and the thrill of winning.

The more you uncover your own *whys*, the closer you'll be to discovering important clues about the kinds of work that are best for you.

Big Activity #2: **what are your interests and strengths?**

things you enjoy doing	why you enjoy doing them
1	• • •
2	• • •
3	• • •

Big Question #3:
what are your work values?

Chances are, you've never given a moment's thought to this next question. At least not in the context of career planning.

You already looked at who you are and what you enjoy and do well. The idea being, of course, to seek out career options that make the most of your innate qualities, preferences, and natural abilities.

As you start checking into various careers, you'll discover one more dimension associated with making personally appropriate career choices. You'll find that even though people may have the exact same job title, they may execute their jobs in dramatically different ways. For instance, everyone knows about teachers. They teach things to other people. Period.

But wait. If you line up 10 aspiring teachers in one room, you may be surprised to discover how vastly different their interpretations of the job may be. There are the obvious differences, of course. One may want to teach young children; one may want to teach adults. One will focus on teaching math, while another one focuses on teaching Spanish.

Look a little closer and you'll find even greater disparity in the choices they make. One may opt for the prestige (and paycheck) of working in an Ivy League college, while another is completely committed to teaching disadvantaged children in a remote area of the Appalachian Mountains. One may approach teaching simply as a way to make a living, while another devotes almost every waking hour to working with his or her students.

These subtle but significant differences reflect what's truly important to each person. In a word, they reflect the person's values—those things that are most important to them.

People's values depend on many factors—their upbringing, their life experiences, their goals and ambitions, their religious beliefs, and, quite frankly, the way they view the world and their role in it. Very few people share exactly the same values. However, that doesn't necessarily mean that some people are right and others are wrong. It just means they have different perspectives.

Here's a story that shows how different values can be reflected in career choices.

Imagine: It's five years after college graduation and a group of college friends are back together for the first time. They catch up about their lives, their families, and their careers. Listen in on one of their reunion conversations and see if you can guess what each is doing now.

Alice: I have the best career. Every day I get the chance to help kids with special needs get a good education.

Bob: I love my career, too. It's great to know that I am making my town a safer place for everyone.

Cathy: It was tough for me to commit to more school after college. But I'm glad I did. After all I went through when my parents divorced, I'm glad I can be there to make things easier for other families.

David: I know how you feel. I'm glad I get to do something that helps companies function smoothly and keep our economy strong. Of course, you remember that I had a hard time deciding whether to pursue this career or teaching! This way I get the best of both worlds.

Elizabeth: It's great that we both ended up in the corporate world. You know that I was always intrigued by the stock market.

So exactly what is each of the five former freshman friends doing today? Have you made your guesses?

Alice is a lawyer. She specializes in education law. She makes sure that school districts provide special needs children with all of the resources they are entitled to under the law.

Bob is a lawyer. He is a prosecuting attorney and makes his town safer by ensuring that justice is served when someone commits a crime.

Cathy is a lawyer. She practices family law. She helps families negotiate separation and divorce agreements and makes sure that adoption and custody proceedings protect everyone involved. Sometimes she even provides legal intervention to protect adults or children who are in abusive situations.

David is a lawyer. He practices employment law. He helps companies set up policies that follow fair employment practices. He also gives seminars to managers, teaching them what the law says and means about sexual harassment, discrimination, and termination of employment.

Elizabeth is a lawyer. She practices corporate law and is indispensable to corporations with legal responsibilities towards stockholders and the government.

Wow! All five friends have the same job title. But each describes his/her job so differently! All five were able to enter the field of law and focus on the things that are most important to them: quality education, freedom from crime, protection of families and children, fairness in the workplace, and corporate economic growth. Identifying and honoring your personal values is an important part of choosing your life's work.

Big Activity #3:
what are your work values?

Step 1: Look at the following chart. If this book doesn't belong to you, divide a sheet of paper into the following three columns:

- **Essential**

  Statements that fall into this column are very important to you. If the job doesn't satisfy these needs, you're not interested.

- **Okay**

  Great if the job satisfies these needs, but you can also live without them.

- **No Way**

  Statements that fall into this column represent needs that are not at all important to you or things you'd rather do without or simply couldn't tolerate.

Step 2: Look over the following list of statements representing different work values. Rewrite each statement in the appropriate column. Does the first statement represent something that is critical to you to have in your work? If so, write it in the first column. No big deal either way? Write it in the second column. Couldn't stand it? Write it in the third column. Repeat the same process for each of the value statements.

Step 3: When you're finished, place your complete work values chart in your Big Question AnswerBook.

Got it? Then get with it.

Really think about these issues. Lay it on the line. What values are so deeply ingrained in you that you'd be absolutely miserable if you had to sacrifice them for a job? Religious beliefs and political leanings fall into this category for some people.

Which ones provide room for some give and take? Things like vacation and benefits, working hours, and other issues along those lines may be completely negotiable for some people, but absolutely not for others.

Just remember, wherever you go and whatever you do, be sure that the choices you make are true to you.

Big Activity #3: **what are your work values?**

work values	essential	okay	no way
1. I can count on plenty of opportunity for advancement and taking on more responsibility.			
2. I can work to my fullest potential using all of my abilities.			
3. I would be able to give directions and instructions to others.			
4. I would always know exactly what my manager expects of me.			
5. I could structure my own day.			
6. I would be very busy all day.			
7. I would work in attractive and pleasant surroundings.			
8. My coworkers would be people I might choose as friends.			
9. I would get frequent feedback about my performance.			
10. I could continue my education to progress to an even higher level job.			
11. Most of the time I would be able to work alone.			
12. I would know precisely what I need to do to succeed at the job.			
13. I could make decisions on my own.			

Big Activity #3: **what are your work values?**

work values	essential	okay	no way
14. I would have more than the usual amount of vacation time.			
15. I would be working doing something I really believe in.			
16. I would feel like part of a team.			
17. I would find good job security and stable employment opportunities in the industry.			
18. I could depend on my manager for the training I need.			
19. I would earn lots of money.			
20. I would feel a sense of accomplishment in my work.			
21. I would be helping other people.			
22. I could try out my own ideas.			
23. I would not need to have further training or education to do this job.			
24. I would get to travel a lot.			
25. I could work the kind of hours I need to balance work, family, and personal responsibilities.			

To summarize in my own words, the work values most important to me include:

Big Question #4:
what is your work personality?

Congratulations. After completing the first three activities, you've already discovered a set of skills you can use throughout your life. Basing key career decisions on factors associated with who you are, what you enjoy and do well, and what's most important about work will help you today as you're just beginning to explore the possibilities, as well as into the future as you look for ways to cultivate your career.

Now that you've got that mastered, let's move on to another important skill. This one blends some of what you just learned about yourself with what you need to learn about the real world of work. It's a reality check of sorts as you align and merge your personal interests and abilities with those required in different work situations. At the end of this task you will identify your personal interest profile.

This activity is based on the work of Dr. John Holland. Dr. Holland conducted groundbreaking research that identified different characteristics in people. He found that he could classify people into six basic groups based on which characteristics tended to occur at the same time. He also found that the characteristics that defined the different groups of people were also characteristics that corresponded to success in different groups of occupations. The result of all that work was a classification system that identifies and names six distinct groups of people who share personal interests or characteristics and are likely to be successful in a group of clearly identified jobs.

Dr. Holland's work is respected by workforce professionals everywhere and is widely used by employers and employment agencies to help people get a handle on the best types of work to pursue.

The following Work Interest Profiler (WIP) is based on Dr. Holland's theories and was developed by the U.S. Department of Labor's Employment and Training Administration as part of an important project called O*Net. O*Net is a system used in all 50 states to provide career and employment services to thousands of people every year. It's a system you'll want to know about when it's time to take that first plunge into the world of work. If you'd like, you can find more information about this system at ***http://online.onetcenter.org***.

Big Activity #4:
what is your work personality?

By completing O*Net's Work Interest Profiler (WIP), you'll gain valuable insight into the types of work that are right for you.

here's how it works

The WIP lists many activities that real people do at real jobs. Your task is to read a brief statement about each of these activities and decide if it is something you think you'd enjoy doing. Piece of cake!

Don't worry about whether you have enough education or training to perform the activity. And, for now, forget about how much money you would make performing the activity.

Just boil it down to whether or not you'd like performing each work activity. If you'd like it, put a check in the *like* column that corresponds to each of the six interest areas featured in the test on the handy dandy chart you're about to create (or use the one in the book if it's yours). If you don't like it, put that check in the *dislike* column. What if you don't have a strong opinion on a particular activity? That's okay. Count that one as *unsure*.

Be completely honest with yourself. No one else is going to see your chart. If you check things you think you "should" check, you are not helping yourself find the career that will make you happy.

Before you start, create a chart for yourself. Your scoring sheet will have six horizontal rows and three vertical columns. Label the six rows as Sections 1 through 6, and label the three columns *like*, *dislike*, and *unsure*.

how to complete the Work Interest Profiler

Step 1: Start with Section 1.

Step 2: Look at the first activity and decide whether you would like to do it as part of your job.

Step 3: Put a mark in the appropriate column (*Like*, *Dislike*, or *Unsure*) on the Section 1 row.

Step 4: Continue for every activity in Section 1. Then do Sections 2 through 6.

Step 5: When you've finished all of the sections, count the number of marks you have in each column and write down the total.

Remember, this is not a test! There are no right or wrong answers. You are completing this profile to learn more about yourself and your work-related interests.

Also, once you've completed this activity, be sure to put your chart and any notes in your Big Question AnswerBook.

Ready? Let's go!

Section 1

1. Drive a taxi
2. Repair household appliances
3. Catch fish as a member of a fishing crew
4. Paint houses
5. Assemble products in a factory
6. Install flooring in houses
7. Perform lawn care services
8. Drive a truck to deliver packages to homes and offices
9. Work on an offshore oil-drilling rig
10. Put out forest fires
11. Fix a broken faucet
12. Refinish furniture
13. Guard money in an armored car
14. Lay brick or tile
15. Operate a dairy farm
16. Raise fish in a fish hatchery
17. Build a brick walkway
18. Enforce fish and game laws
19. Assemble electronic parts
20. Build kitchen cabinets
21. Maintain the grounds of a park
22. Operate a motorboat to carry passengers
23. Set up and operate machines to make products
24. Spray trees to prevent the spread of harmful insects
25. Monitor a machine on an assembly line

Section 2

1. Study space travel
2. Develop a new medicine
3. Study the history of past civilizations
4. Develop a way to better predict the weather
5. Determine the infection rate of a new disease
6. Study the personalities of world leaders
7. Investigate the cause of a fire
8. Develop psychological profiles of criminals
9. Study whales and other types of marine life
10. Examine blood samples using a microscope
11. Invent a replacement for sugar
12. Study genetics
13. Do research on plants or animals
14. Study weather conditions
15. Investigate crimes
16. Study ways to reduce water pollution
17. Develop a new medical treatment or procedure
18. Diagnose and treat sick animals
19. Conduct chemical experiments
20. Study rocks and minerals
21. Do laboratory tests to identify diseases
22. Study the structure of the human body
23. Plan a research study
24. Study the population growth of a city
25. Make a map of the bottom of the ocean

Section 3

1. Paint sets for a play
2. Create special effects for movies
3. Write reviews of books or movies
4. Compose or arrange music
5. Design artwork for magazines
6. Pose for a photographer
7. Create dance routines for a show
8. Play a musical instrument
9. Edit movies
10. Sing professionally
11. Announce a radio show
12. Perform stunts for a movie or television show
13. Design sets for plays
14. Act in a play
15. Write a song
16. Perform jazz or tap dance
17. Sing in a band
18. Direct a movie
19. Write scripts for movies or television shows
20. Audition singers and musicians for a musical show
21. Conduct a musical choir
22. Perform comedy routines in front of an audience
23. Dance in a Broadway show
24. Perform as an extra in movies, plays, or television shows
25. Write books or plays

Section 4

1. Teach children how to play sports
2. Help people with family-related problems
3. Teach an individual an exercise routine
4. Perform nursing duties in a hospital
5. Help people with personal or emotional problems
6. Teach work and living skills to people with disabilities
7. Assist doctors in treating patients
8. Work with juveniles on probation
9. Supervise the activities of children at a camp
10. Teach an elementary school class
11. Perform rehabilitation therapy
12. Help elderly people with their daily activities
13. Help people who have problems with drugs or alcohol
14. Teach a high school class
15. Give career guidance to people
16. Do volunteer work at a non-profit organization
17. Help families care for ill relatives
18. Teach sign language to people with hearing disabilities
19. Help people with disabilities improve their daily living skills
20. Help conduct a group therapy session
21. Work with children with mental disabilities
22. Give CPR to someone who has stopped breathing
23. Provide massage therapy to people
24. Plan exercises for patients with disabilities
25. Counsel people who have a life-threatening illness

Section 5

1. Sell CDs and tapes at a music store
2. Manage a clothing store
3. Sell houses
4. Sell computer equipment in a store
5. Operate a beauty salon or barber shop
6. Sell automobiles
7. Represent a client in a lawsuit
8. Negotiate business contracts
9. Sell a soft drink product line to stores and restaurants
10. Start your own business
11. Be responsible for the operations of a company
12. Give a presentation about a product you are selling
13. Buy and sell land
14. Sell restaurant franchises to individuals
15. Manage the operations of a hotel
16. Negotiate contracts for professional athletes
17. Sell merchandise at a department store
18. Market a new line of clothing
19. Buy and sell stocks and bonds
20. Sell merchandise over the telephone
21. Run a toy store
22. Sell hair-care products to stores and salons
23. Sell refreshments at a movie theater
24. Manage a retail store
25. Sell telephone and other communication equipment

Section 6

1. Develop an office filing system
2. Generate the monthly payroll checks for an office
3. Proofread records or forms
4. Schedule business conferences
5. Enter information into a database
6. Photocopy letters and reports
7. Keep inventory records
8. Record information from customers applying for charge accounts
9. Load computer software into a large computer network
10. Use a computer program to generate customer bills
11. Develop a spreadsheet using computer software
12. Operate a calculator
13. Direct or transfer office phone calls
14. Use a word processor to edit and format documents
15. Transfer funds between banks, using a computer
16. Compute and record statistical and other numerical data
17. Stamp, sort, and distribute office mail
18. Maintain employee records
19. Record rent payments
20. Keep shipping and receiving records
21. Keep accounts payable/receivable for an office
22. Type labels for envelopes and packages
23. Calculate the wages of employees
24. Take notes during a meeting
25. Keep financial records

Section 1
Realistic

	Like	Dislike	Unsure
1.			
2.			
3.			
4.			
5.			
6.			
7.			
8.			
9.			
10.			
11.			
12.			
13.			
14.			
15.			
16.			
17.			
18.			
19.			
20.			
21.			
22.			
23.			
24.			
25.			

Total Realistic

Section 2
Investigative

	Like	Dislike	Unsure
1.			
2.			
3.			
4.			
5.			
6.			
7.			
8.			
9.			
10.			
11.			
12.			
13.			
14.			
15.			
16.			
17.			
18.			
19.			
20.			
21.			
22.			
23.			
24.			
25.			

Total Investigative

Section 3
Artistic

	Like	Dislike	Unsure
1.			
2.			
3.			
4.			
5.			
6.			
7.			
8.			
9.			
10.			
11.			
12.			
13.			
14.			
15.			
16.			
17.			
18.			
19.			
20.			
21.			
22.			
23.			
24.			
25.			

Total Artistic

Section 4
Social

	Like	Dislike	Unsure
1.			
2.			
3.			
4.			
5.			
6.			
7.			
8.			
9.			
10.			
11.			
12.			
13.			
14.			
15.			
16.			
17.			
18.			
19.			
20.			
21.			
22.			
23.			
24.			
25.			

Total Social

Section 5
Enterprising

	Like	Dislike	Unsure
1.			
2.			
3.			
4.			
5.			
6.			
7.			
8.			
9.			
10.			
11.			
12.			
13.			
14.			
15.			
16.			
17.			
18.			
19.			
20.			
21.			
22.			
23.			
24.			
25.			

Total Enterprising

Section 6
Conventional

	Like	Dislike	Unsure
1.			
2.			
3.			
4.			
5.			
6.			
7.			
8.			
9.			
10.			
11.			
12.			
13.			
14.			
15.			
16.			
17.			
18.			
19.			
20.			
21.			
22.			
23.			
24.			
25.			

Total Conventional

What are your top three work personalities? List them here if this is your own book or on a separate piece of paper if it's not.

1. _____
2. _____
3. _____

all done? let's see what it means

Be sure you count up the number of marks in each column on your scoring sheet and write down the total for each column. You will probably notice that you have a lot of *like*s for some sections, and a lot of *dislike*s for other sections. The section that has the most *like*s is your primary interest area. The section with the next highest number of *like*s is your second interest area. The next highest is your third interest area.

Now that you know your top three interest areas, what does it mean about your work personality type? We'll get to that in a minute, but first we are going to answer a couple of other questions that might have crossed your mind:

- What is the best work personality to have?
- What does my work personality mean?

First of all, there is no "best" personality in general. There is, however, a "best" personality for each of us. It's who we really are and how we feel most comfortable. There may be several "best" work personalities for any job because different people may approach the job in different ways. But there is no "best work personality."

Asking about the "best work personality" is like asking whether the "best" vehicle is a sports car, a sedan, a station wagon, or a sports utility vehicle. It all depends on who you are and what you need.

One thing we do know is that our society needs all of the work personalities in order to function effectively. Fortunately, we usually seem to have a good mix of each type.

So, while many people may find science totally boring, there are many other people who find it fun and exciting. Those are the people who invent new technologies, who become doctors and researchers, and who turn natural resources into the things we use every day. Many people may think that spending a day with young children is unbearable, but those who love that environment are the teachers, community leaders, and museum workers that nurture children's minds and personalities.

When everything is in balance, there's a job for every person and a person for every job.

Now we'll get to your work personality. Following are descriptions of each of Dr. Holland's six work personalities that correspond to the six sections in your last exercise. You, like most people, are a unique combination of more than one. A little of this, a lot of that. That's what makes us interesting.

Identify your top three work personalities. Also, pull out your responses to the first three exercises we did. As you read about your top three work personalities, see how they are similar to the way you described yourself earlier.

Type 1
Realistic

Realistic people are often seen as the "Doers." They have mechanical or athletic ability and enjoy working outdoors.

Realistic people like work activities that include practical, hands-on problems and solutions. They enjoy dealing with plants, animals, and real-life materials like wood, tools, and machinery.

Careers that involve a lot of paperwork or working closely with others are usually not attractive to realistic people.

Who you are:
independent
reserved
practical
mechanical
athletic
persistent

What you like to do/what you do well:
build things
train animals
play a sport
fix things
garden
hunt or fish
woodworking
repair cars
refinish furniture

Career possibilities:
aerospace engineer
aircraft pilot
animal breeder
architect
baker/chef
building inspector
carpenter
chemical engineer
civil engineer
construction manager
dental assistant
detective
glazier
jeweler
machinist
oceanographer
optician
park ranger
plumber
police officer
practical nurse
private investigator
radiologist
sculptor

Type 2
Investigative

Investigative people are often seen as the "Thinkers." They much prefer searching for facts and figuring out problems mentally to doing physical activity or leading other people.

If Investigative is one of your strong interest areas, your answers to the earlier exercises probably matched some of these:

Who you are:
curious
logical
independent
analytical
observant
inquisitive

What you like to do/what you do well:
think abstractly
solve problems
use a microscope
do research
fly a plane
explore new subjects
study astronomy
do puzzles
work with a computer

Career possibilities:

aerospace engineer
archaeologist
CAD technician
chemist
chiropractor
computer programmer
coroner
dentist
electrician
ecologist
geneticist
hazardous waste technician
historian
horticulturist
management consultant
medical technologist
meteorologist
nurse practitioner
pediatrician
pharmacist
political scientist
psychologist
software engineer
surgeon
technical writer
veterinarian
zoologist

Type 3
Artistic

Artistic people are the "Creators." People with this primary interest like work activities that deal with the artistic side of things.

Artistic people need to have the opportunity for self-expression in their work. They want to be able to use their imaginations and prefer to work in less structured environments, without clear sets of rules about how things should be done.

Who you are:

imaginative
intuitive
expressive
emotional
creative
independent

What you like to do/what you do well:

draw
paint
play an instrument
visit museums
act
design clothes or rooms
read fiction
travel
write stories, poetry, or music

Career possibilities:

architect
actor
animator
art director
cartoonist
choreographer
costume designer
composer
copywriter
dancer
disc jockey
drama teacher
emcee
fashion designer
graphic designer
illustrator
interior designer
journalist
landscape architect
medical illustrator
photographer
producer
scriptwriter
set designer

Type 4
Social

Social people are known as the "Helpers." They are interested in work that can assist others and promote learning and personal development.

Communication with other people is very important to those in the Social group. They usually do not enjoy jobs that require a great amount of work with objects, machines, or data. Social people like to teach, give advice, help, cure, or otherwise be of service to people.

Who you are:
friendly
outgoing
empathic
persuasive
idealistic
generous

What you like to do/what you do well:
teach others
work in groups
play team sports
care for children
go to parties
help or advise others
meet new people

express yourself
join clubs or organizations

Career possibilities:
animal trainer
arbitrator
art teacher
art therapist
audiologist
child care worker
clergy person
coach
counselor/therapist
cruise director
dental hygienist
employment interviewer
EMT worker
fitness trainer
flight attendant
occupational therapist
police officer
recreational therapist
registered nurse
school psychologist
social worker
substance abuse counselor
teacher
tour guide

Type 5
Enterprising

Enterprising work personalities can be called the "Persuaders." These people like work activities that have to do with starting up and carrying out projects, especially business ventures. They like taking risks for profit, enjoy being responsible for making decisions, and generally prefer action to thought or analysis.

People in the Enterprising group like to work with other people. While the Social group focuses on helping other people, members of the Enterprising group are able to lead, manage, or persuade other people to accomplish the goals of the organization.

Who you are:
assertive
self-confident
ambitious
extroverted
optimistic
adventurous

What you like to do/what you do well:
organize activities
sell things
promote ideas

discuss politics
hold office in clubs
give talks or speeches
meet people
initiate projects
start your own business

Career possibilities:
advertising
chef
coach, scout
criminal investigator
economist
editor
foreign service officer
funeral director
hotel manager
journalist
lawyer
lobbyist
public relations specialist
newscaster
restaurant manager
sales manager
school principal
ship's captain
stockbroker
umpire, referee
urban planner

Type 6
Conventional

People in the Conventional group are the "Organizers." They like work activities that follow set procedures and routines. They are more comfortable and proficient working with data and detail than they are with generalized ideas.

Conventional people are happiest in work situations where the lines of authority are clear, where they know exactly what responsibilities are expected of them, and where there are precise standards for the work.

Who you are:
well-organized
accurate
practical
persistent
conscientious
ambitious

What you like to do/what you do well:
work with numbers
type accurately
collect or organize things
follow up on tasks
be punctual
be responsible for details
proofread

keep accurate records
understand regulations

Career possibilities:
accountant
actuary
air traffic controller
assessor
budget analyst
building inspector
chief financial officer
corporate treasurer
cost estimator
court reporter
economist
environmental compliance lawyer
fire inspector
insurance underwriter
legal secretary
mathematician
medical secretary
proofreader
tax preparer

architecture and construction careers work personality codes

Once you've discovered your own unique work personality code, you can use it to explore the careers profiled in this book and elsewhere. Do keep in mind though that this code is just a tool meant to help focus your search. It's not meant to box you in or to keep you from pursuing any career that happens to capture your imagination.

Following is a chart listing the work personality codes associated with each of the careers profiled in this book.

	Realistic	Investigative	Artistic	Social	Enterprising	Conventional
My Work Personality Code (mark your top three areas)						
Architect	X	X	X			
Boilermaker	X			X	X	
Brick Mason		X		X	X	
Building Inspector		X		X		X
Carpenter	X				X	X
Cement Mason	X				X	X
Civil Engineer	X	X			X	
Construction Foreman	X			X	X	
Construction Manager	X			X	X	
Demolition Engineer	X			X	X	
Drafter	X			X	X	
Electrician	X			X	X	
Environmental Engineer	X	X			X	
Equipment Manager	X			X	X	
Estimator	X				X	X
Flooring Mechanic	X	X			X	
General Contractor	X	X			X	
Glazier	X			X	X	

My Work Personality Code	Realistic	Investigative	Artistic	Social	Enterprising	Conventional
Heating, Ventilating, and Air-conditioning Technician	X			X	X	
Heavy Equipment Operator	X	X			X	
Highway Maintenance Worker	X				X	X
Interior Designer	X		X		X	
Ironworker	X			X		X
Landscape Architect	X	X	X			
Mechanical Engineer	X	X			X	
Painter	X			X		X
Plasterer and Drywall Installer	X			X	X	
Plumber	X	X			X	
Preservationist	X	X	X			
Roofer	X				X	X
Safety Director		X		X	X	
Scheduler	X	X			X	
Surveyor	X	X			X	
Urban Planner		X		X	X	
Wastewater Maintenance Technician	X			X	X	

Now it's time to move on to the next big step in the Big Question process. While the first step focused on you, the next one focuses on the world of work. It includes profiles of a wide variety of occupations related to architecture and construction, a roundtable discussion with professionals working in these fields, and a mind-boggling list of other careers to consider when wanting to blend passion or talent in these areas with your life's work.

explore your options

By now you probably have a fairly good understanding of the assets (some fully realized and perhaps others only partially developed) that you bring to your future career. You've defined key characteristics about yourself, identified special interests and strengths, examined your work values, and analyzed your basic work personality traits. All in all, you've taken a good, hard look at yourself and we're hoping that you're encouraged by all the potential you've discovered.

In this section, you'll have the opportunity to explore a wide variety of careers in the construction and architecture industry. These careers include everything involved in designing, planning, building, and maintaining the built environment—whether the structure is brand new, "historically" old, or in need of repair or expansion. With well over 13 million jobs, construction and architecture represent one of the largest industries in America.

Perhaps more than any other industry, this one offers challenging and interesting opportunities for hands-on learning through on-the-job training and apprenticeships. Obtaining a skilled trade in this way paves the way for high school graduates to find well-paying, high-demand employment. In fact, growing numbers of high schools offer construction career "academies" where students can gain experience and earn credentials that prepare them for either gainful employment or advanced training opportunities upon graduation.

fyi Each of the following profiles includes several common elements to help guide you through an effective career exploration process. For each career, you'll find

- A sidebar loaded with information you can use to find out more about the profession. Professional associations, pertinent reading materials, the low-down on wages and suggested training requirements, and a list of typical types of employers are all included to give you a broader view of what the career is all about.
- An informative essay describing what the career involves.
- Get Started Now strategies you can use right now to get prepared, test the waters, and develop your skills.
- A Hire Yourself project providing realistic activities like those you would actually find on the job. Try these learning activities and find out what it's really like to be a . . . you name it.

You don't have to read the profiles in order. You may want to first browse through the career ideas that appear to be most interesting. Then check out the others—you never know what might interest you when you know more about it. As you read each profile, think about how well it matches up with what you learned about yourself in Section 1: **Discover You at Work.** Narrow down your options to a few careers and use the rating system described below to evaluate your interest levels.

- **No way!** There's not even a remote chance that this career is a good fit for me. (Since half of figuring out what you do want to do in life involves figuring out what you don't want to do, this is not a bad place to be.)
- **This is intriguing.** I want to learn more about it and look at similar careers as well. (The activities outlined in Section 3: **Experiment with Success** will be especially useful in this regard.)
- **This is it!** It's the career I've been looking for all my life and I want to go after it with all I've got. (Head straight to Section 3: **Experiment with Success.**)

Of course, there's also plenty of demand for those with college degrees too. In fact, due to the large number of baby boomers expected to retire over the next 10 years, the construction industry is actively seeking the "best and the brightest" of your generation to join their ranks, learn the ropes, and get ready to eventually assume roles at the highest levels of responsibility.

Even if choosing a career in construction has never crossed your mind, take a good look at the opportunities presented here. You may be surprised to discover that this is an industry likely to offer something for just about everyone.

In the following section, you'll find in-depth profiles of 35 careers representing the construction and architecture industries. Some of these careers you may already know about. Others will present new ideas for your consideration. All are part of a dynamic and important segment of the U.S. economy.

To make it easier to find careers that interest you, the U.S. Department of Education established three pathways that group occupations according to common knowledge and skill requirements. These pathways are design and pre-construction, construction, and maintenance and operations. Following are descriptions of each pathway.

Design and Pre-construction

Great ideas provide the framework for this pathway. Professionals in these occupations turn ideas into full-blown plans that other professionals use throughout the building process—*planning* being the single best word to describe the work associated with this pathway. Design and pre-construction careers profiled in this book include architect, civil engineer, drafter, environmental engineer, estimator, interior designer, landscape architect, mechanical engineer, preservationist, scheduler, surveyor, and urban planner.

Construction

Those involved in construction actually build our homes, schools, buildings, highways, streets, bridges, tunnels, airports, power plants, and any other structure you could possibly imagine. Construction careers profiled in this book include brick mason, carpenter, cement mason, construction foreman, construction manager, electrician, flooring mechanic, general contractor, glazier, heavy equipment operator, HVAC (heating, ventilating, and air-conditioning) technician, ironworker, painter, plasterer and drywall installer, plumber, and roofer.

A Note on Websites

Websites tend to move around a bit. If you have trouble finding a particular site, use an Internet browser to search for a specific website or type of information.

Maintenance and Operations

These behind-the-scenes occupations keep construction projects on track and running smoothly. They include the professionals who unload, inspect, and repair equipment and machinery as well as those who order supplies and handle the business and administrative task associated with any construction project. Maintenance and operations careers profiled in this book include boilermaker, building inspector, demolition engineer, equipment manager, highway maintenance worker, safety director, and wastewater maintenance technician.

As you explore the 35 careers profiled in this book and others in this series, remember to keep what you've learned about yourself in mind. Consider each option in light of what you know about your interests, strengths, work values, and work personality.

Pay close attention to the job requirements. Does it require math aptitude? Good writing skills? Ability to take things apart and visualize how they go back together? If you don't have the necessary abilities (and don't have a strong desire to acquire them), you probably won't enjoy the job.

For instance, several popular TV shows make forensic investigation look like a fascinating career. And it is—for some people. But when considering whether forensic investigation—or any career for that matter—is right for you, think about the skills it takes to succeed. In this case, we're talking about lots of chemistry, anatomy, and physics. And, quite frankly, working with dead people. Be realistic about each profession so that you can make an honest assessment about how appropriate it is for you.

architect

Einstein said once that he thought in shapes and images instead of words. He might have made a great architect! Architects are licensed professionals who design skyscrapers, museums, airports, homes, and other buildings by taking an idea or concept and turning it into a meticulously detailed drawing or plan that, with the help of all kinds of other construction professionals, eventually becomes a finished product. This is not to say, however, that you have to be Einstein to be an architect. But you must be willing to undergo years of education and training.

Architects must create buildings that are not only aesthetically pleasing but structurally sound, and fitting to their purpose (for instance, a museum might require a series of connecting rooms and several levels). Architects do not disappear into an office, draw up a draft (design), and hand it over, finished. They must lay out their ideas with the client, and

Search It!
The American Institute of Architects at **www.aia.org**

Read It!
Architectural Record at **www.archrecord.construction.com**

Learn It!
- A professional degree in architecture is required, either by completing a five-year bachelor's program or by obtaining both a bachelor's and a master's
- For a list of schools, visit the National Architectural Accrediting Board website at **www.naab.org**

Earn It!
Median annual salary is $56,620. (Source: U.S. Department of Labor)

Find It!
Architects are recruited by individuals, large firms, and government agencies. Check out potential employers at **http://aia.jobcontrolcenter.com/search.cfm**.

Get Started Now!

Use these strategies to get ready for a future in architecture:

- Architecture is a unique profession that blends art with practicality. Do some research and read about the vision and designs of great architects such as Frank Gehry, Rem Koolhaas, I.M. Pei, and Frank Lloyd Wright. Review photos of their structures, and jot down notes about what you like and dislike about their designs. A good place to start is **http://buildings.greatbuildings.com**.
- Math classes are essential—take as many as you can. But it also helps to take history, art, English, and science classes too.
- Take a computer science class through your high school or at a community college, especially a class in computer drafting.

Hire Yourself

Architectural firms are always looking for innovative thinkers. To be considered for an entry-level position at Future Homes Inc, the human resources department wants to see a simple drawing detailing a home of the future. Your design should show innovations you'd like to see in bathrooms, bedrooms, kitchens, living rooms, and other standard rooms of a house. Put your ideas to paper in a drawing and write a brief explanation of the innovations in each room.

often sell the client on a vision. That's why the successful architect knows not only how to articulate his vision well on paper, but in person as well. It helps to be "people-savvy" in this field.

When a proposal is sold, the architect can then begin to draft final building plans that detail both appearance and construction. This plan includes the design, plus everything that will make the structure work: heating, ventilating, and air-conditioning (HVAC) systems, wiring, plumbing, and so on. Architects must also abide by building and zoning codes when drafting. In the past, drafting meant creating detailed drawings with pencil and paper, but today's computer-assisted design and drafting (CADD) technology speeds the process and architects more easily envision different structures with the help of a computer.

In addition to designing a building, the architect may help a client with the logistics of the project: collecting bids from construction companies, hiring contractors, and negotiating contracts. He or she may also go on-site to see that construction remains faithful to his design, and that it does so using the proper materials, in a timely manner and within budget.

Some architects choose to specialize either in a stage of the building process, or in a particular type. For instance, an architect may work primarily as a consultant in the pre-construction, or planning, stage. Alternately, he or she may work purely on-site, to ensure the project runs according to plan. Some see all their projects from start to finish, but only build one type—split-level houses, for instance.

Fortunately, as construction projects are expected to grow in the immediate future, so are the opportunities for new architects. Those possessing both artistic flair and proficiencies in math and science may want to take a closer look at this profession.

find your boilermaker future

boilermaker

If you live in a home that keeps you warm and cozy during the winter months, you may have a boilermaker to thank. Boilermakers are experts at making, installing, and repairing the boilers that heat houses, apartments, and office buildings. Simply put, boilers are metal vessels that hold water that can be heated to produce steam. The steam can be used not only to produce heat but also to operate huge turbines in electric powerplants and to run engines on ships and trains. In addition to boilers, these specialized workers also make vats and tanks that are used to hold other substances, such as chemicals and oil.

In some ways, building a boiler is like doing a giant 3-D puzzle or model. Boilers are made piece by piece. Each piece of a boiler is cast (formed) out of molten (melted) iron or steel. Then, referring to a blueprint, which gives very precise measurements and lists all components, boilermakers accurately position parts using implements like straightedges, tape measures, levels, and squares. To measure depth and verticality, they use a plumb line (a cord with a weight at one end). After

Search It!
The Boilermakers Union at
www.boilermakers.org

Read It!
The Boilermaker Reporter on-line at
www.boilermakers.org/
6-Reporter/6-index.html

Learn It!
- On-the-job training or trade school required
- Formal apprenticeship optional: includes four years of training on the job and a minimum of 144 hours of classroom instruction

Earn It!
Median annual salary is $42,000.
(Source: U.S. Department of Labor)

Find It!
Boilermakers can find work with major boiler manufacturers like Hurst Boiler &Welding Co. (*www.hurstboiler.com/employment.htm*) and ENERFAB (*www.enerfab.com*), as well as with heavy construction companies and plumbing, heating, and air-conditioning companies.

Get Started Now!

Use these strategies to get ready for a future as a boilermaker:

- Read more on the industry at Boilermakers National Apprenticeship Program at *www.bnap.com/career.htm*.
- Math, science, and metal shop classes can give you the right background.
- Some high schools offer youth apprenticeship programs that allow students to go off campus. If you are interested, talk to your guidance counselor to see if this is an option.

Hire Yourself

A local trade school is teaching a course on boilermaking, and you've been hired as a teaching assistant. Your first assignment is to show students the basic components of a boiler. Create a poster featuring simple illustrations of different basic boiler types and illustrate the basic components—valves, gauges, etc. Use information like that found at the How Stuff Works website at *www.travel. howstuffworks.com/steam2.htm* and the Aalborg Industries *www.aalborgindustries.com/ifs/files/AI/eng/Presentation/Website/Marine/ Manufacturing/process.jsp* to get started. An on-line search using your favorite Internet search engine (such as Google or Yahoo) will help you find additional resources.

plates are aligned and excess materials are cut, these skilled workers position and weld together the parts. Increasingly, manufacturers rely on automated welding machines, since they are more efficient and tend to produce a more exact final product.

The resulting container has to withstand high-pressure from water that is heated to 212 degrees Fahrenheit. That pressure can be equivalent to being sat on by five elephants! But if the pressure goes too high a boiler can break down or even explode. That's why boilermakers attach valves and gauges in order to monitor and maintain the proper amounts of pressure.

Some of the biggest boilers weigh many tons and have to be put into place using heaving rigging and cranes. However, the final assembly of a large boiler often occurs on site. Positioning is very important. If placed incorrectly or off-balance, a vessel may not be able to maintain a high pressure and may be prone to break. To ensure safety, all U.S. boilers must meet standards set forth in the American Society of Mechanical Engineers' Boiler Construction Code.

When boilers do break, boilermakers come to the rescue. They make repairs using hammers and torches to reshape bent legs or valves; they fix insulation by laying cement; they replace worn parts, such as burners, to make a vessel more efficient; they clean containers with solvent and wire brushes; and they strengthen joints and stop up holes or leaks. A boiler should last at least 30 years, but during its lifetime it will require a substantial amount of maintenance. After all, it is under constant pressure!

The conditions under which a boilermaker works are not for the faint of heart (or body). He or she is often laboring in hot temperatures in poorly ventilated spaces, dealing with heavy equipment and machinery. Even though boilers are placed in the basement of an office building or the bottom of a ship, the bigger boilers can require professionals to climb ladders and work at significant heights. Because of this challenging work environment, boilermakers typically wear protective clothing, hardhats, safety glasses, shoes, and even respirators to get enough air. To bargain for better work conditions, as well as wages and benefits, boilermakers typically belong to a union.

For those interested in becoming a boilermaker, two to four years of on-the-job training is the only hard-and-fast requirement, but employers prefer to hire those who have completed high school. You can also enroll in a trade school that offers courses in blueprint reading, and instruction in how to use the instruments used in boilermaking (welding torches and rigging, for instance).

Search It!
Masonry Contractors Association of America at ***www. masoncontractors.org*** and the International Union of Bricklayers at ***www.bacweb. org/bachome.htm***

Read It!
Masonry Magazine at ***www.masonrymagazine.com***

Learn It!
● High school diploma
● Skills are learned on-the-job or through formal apprenticeship programs

Earn It!
Median annual salary is $41,828. (Source: U.S. Bureau of Labor Statistics)

Find It!
For information on training and apprenticeships, visit ***http:// imiweb.org/imihome.htm*** or ***www.masoncontractors.org/ masonrycareertraining/ index.html***.

find your brick mason future

brick mason

When people set out to build a structure that will withstand harsh outside elements and stand the test of time, they often turn to brick and stone masons for help. These construction professionals work with some of nature's strongest raw materials—marble, stone, and granite. They represent a long tradition of fine craftsmanship that transcends nearly all cultural and geographic boundaries.

The first responsibility of the brick mason is to study the blueprint design of a structure to determine the number of bricks and their layout. Sometimes, each individual brick is numbered and has a specific place in the structure. Then, they set up the bricks without mortar (the material used to hold them together, made of sand, water, and cement). A nylon line is stretched between corners to ensure the bricks are laid straight and level. Next, the masons set up the corners at the ends of each structure. Finally, the areas between the corners, like walls, are filled in with the bricks and mortar.

Stonemasons, on the other hand, start with a layer of stones set in a layer of mortar. Then, stones are aligned with the use of wedges or an object called a plumb line. The process of layering stones and mortar continues, and the wedges are removed and replaced with more mortar. Sometimes, permanent brackets are used to hold larger stones in place.

Masons use a variety of tools to assist in their work. A plumb rule is a leveling device that helps keep rows of bricks straight. Hammers and chisels are used to cut and shape brick and stone that are too large or

Get Started Now!
● Basic math skills are important.
● Make sure you are in good physical shape and are able to lift heavy objects.
● Shop and mechanical drawing classes can give you the edge you need to succeed.

Hire Yourself!

You're a brick mason. Blueprints for a job call for a 30-foot long and 18-foot wide brick driveway. Each brick is six inches long and three inches high. There is an inch of mortar in between each of the bricks, going across and down. (There is no mortar on the borders of the driveway). How many bricks will be needed, and will any need to be cut?

needs to fit into areas, like corners and borders of windows. Stonemasons use rubber mallets to force stones into place. Additionally, masons need to be adept at mixing and spreading mortar. A large amount of mason work is done outdoors. In addition to walls, masons build patios, walkways, fireplaces, and more. Candidates for this career should be in good physical condition with much heavy lifting and bending required.

A high school diploma is helpful in securing work as a brick or stonemason. While some masons simply learn on-the-job while working as helpers, many enter formal, three-year apprenticeship programs. These programs combine on-the-job training with 144 hours a year of classroom instruction. During their career, a mason may move up the ladder to become a supervisor or even a contractor. Similar jobs include concrete finisher and cement mason. More than 25 percent of masons are self-employed and work on small jobs. While job availability changes with the economy and weather, both new construction and refurbishment work are expected to create job opportunities in this field.

building inspector

If any career should have the motto "safety first," it should be that of the building inspector. The main purpose of his or her job is to make sure buildings are secure according to standards set by both the International Code Council (ICC) and the project developer. The building inspector performs check-ups before construction begins, while construction is in progress, and after a building is completed, ensuring that guidelines are met at each stage. Their work stretches beyond homes and office structures and includes roadways, water systems, dams, and bridges.

Following universal standards established by the ICC, inspectors guard against sloppy, unsafe construction. They also work to ensure that guidelines detailed in a specific project's contract are followed. Inspectors may report their findings using a computer, a paper checklist, or a combination of both.

Before construction on a building begins, building inspectors test the quality and depth of the soil on which the foundation of a structure is set. During construction, they might check fire exits, escapes, sprinklers, and alarm systems, and when construction is finished they perform a final inspection to see that everything is satisfactory. During construction, if violations are not corrected within a certain period of

Search It!
The International Code Council at
www.iccsafe.org

Read It!
Building Safety Journal on-line at
www.iccsafe.org/news/bsj

Learn It!
- High school diploma or GED (general equivalency diploma)
- Coursework at a postsecondary school in engineering or architecture is helpful
- Several years of experience as a construction worker, supervisor, or manager is required

Earn It!
Median annual salary is $41,620. (Source: U.S. Department of Labor)

Find It!
Building inspectors can look for openings on industry-specific job sites like **www.iccsafe.org/ e/listjobs**, or by searching state or local government sites, like the New York City Department of Buildings at **http://nyc.gov/html/ dob/html/jobs.html**.

Get Started Now!
Use these strategies to get ready for a future in building inspection:
- Communication skills—both writing and speaking—are key when identifying problems. Involvement in the school newspaper is a good way to hone these skills.
- Algebra, geometry, and English classes will be helpful.
- Contact your local government to see if you can job shadow a building inspector.

Hire Yourself!

We've already said building inspection is all about identifying problems. Start at school: what may not be quite "up-to-code"? Prepare a list of five things that could use improvement, and how you would fix them. For instance, if stairwells are always traffic-jammed at a particular time, you could propose certain of them be reserved for going upstairs, while alternate ones be used for going down.

time, a "stop work" order may be issued. Anything amiss in the final inspection must be fixed before the project—building, bridge, or whatever is up for inspection—is open for use.

The elements that an inspector checks in a structure can vary from project to project. A building's contract and purpose can determine the standards it must meet. For instance, a public library may have to be wheelchair-accessible, and the inspector may review the blueprints, looking for an entrance with a ramp, or recommend ways to make the library accessible, such as with stairwell lifts. In areas prone to natural disasters like hurricanes or earthquakes, additional safety requirements must be adhered to and inspectors make sure the proper reinforcement goes into these structures.

Inspectors use tools like metering devices that measure the flow of a gas or liquid, tape measures, and concrete strength measurers to evaluate buildings. Their work day is very active since they spend most of their time on-site climbing ladders, riding hoists up several stories, and crawling mole-like along floors and shafts. They take photos, document their findings, and file reports—all of which they deliver to their employer. Employers include state, local, and federal government agencies, as well as private engineering and architectural firms.

Most employers do not require an undergraduate degree, as most of the training is done on the job. However, some government positions require inspectors to pass a civil service exam and certification, such as that offered by the International Code Council. Inspectors must also continue to educate themselves on code status: new ones, outdated ones, revised ones. Over the next decade, opportunities are expected to grow, so if you've ever had an interest in construction and helping the welfare of the public, this may be a perfect career to combine both.

find your carpenter future

Search It!
United Brotherhood of Carpenters and Joiners of America at ***www.carpenters.org***

Read It!
Carpenter Magazine at ***www.carpenters.org/carpentermag***

Learn It!
● Carpenters learn their craft through on-the-job training, trade and vocational schools, and apprenticeships
● For apprentice information, visit ***http://home.att.net/~secrc/training/carp_training.html***

Earn It!
Median annual salary is $34,195. (Source: U.S. Bureau of Labor Statistics)

Find It!
Check out opportunities listed at ***www.carpentry.jobs.helpwantedsite.com***, ***www.myhomeconstruction.com***, and ***http://backstagejobs.com/carp.htm***.

carpenter

What do Jimmy Carter, Harrison Ford, and Jesus Christ all have in common? They've all worked as carpenters—the largest of all the construction trades. Throughout history, carpentry has been a reliable source of income for people—it's always in demand and typically recession-proof.

Carpenters apply their trade on a range of construction projects both big and small. They cut, fit, and assemble wood and other materials for the construction of buildings, highways, bridges, theaters, industrial plants, ships, and many other structures. In television, theater, and film, carpenters work with designers and artistic directors to build sets.

On a typical construction project, a carpenter may be called upon to build stairs, lay wooden floors, put in doorways and windows, or install kitchen cabinets. The work is varied but each job usually involves some similar steps. After checking over blueprints, carpenters make measurements and get their materials ready to build. Although they still depend on the basic age-old tools of hammers and nails, these skilled workers can speed a job along with power tools, such as drills, jigsaws, and sanders. They may also connect materials using screws, adhesives, and

Get Started Now!

A career in carpentry requires building some basic skills now.
● Study math and enroll in shop classes at your school. Classes in industrial arts and mechanical drawing will help you to decide whether you have the aptitude for this line of work.
● After school, apply for apprenticeship training with the local labor-management program of the carpenter's union and the construction contractors.
● Go to your local hobby shop and try a simple woodworking kit to make a birdhouse, or model ship.

Hire Yourself

You have a client who needs a bookshelf built to order to fit a 6' x 4' space, but first he wants to see sketches of what you would build. If you want to go beyond a sketch, you may attempt to create a blueprint—look at some blueprint instructions on-line at *www.jeffgreefwoodworking.com/pc/index.html*. You're certainly not an expert yet, but try and write down the cost of materials, the necessary tools for the job, and the amount of time it will take to complete the project. You may want to get some help from your local hardware or home supply store.

staples. When the job is done, they make sure things are level and aligned with tools such as rules, plumb bobs, and levels.

The work requires an artistic eye, a lot of stamina, and a mastery of the tools and techniques.

Beginners study the craft through on-the-job training and formal apprenticeship programs. Apprentices receive instruction in safety, first aid, blueprint reading, freehand sketching, basic mathematics, and a variety of carpentry techniques. By working on the job as an apprentice, those starting out are often able to land that first entry-level job. To hone more advanced skills, many take courses at vocational school. Carpenters often work as part of a construction team, but many practice their trade alone, working on individual projects such as cabinetmaking, custom furniture building, or home-remodeling.

Professional woodworking can be rewarding in that it combines creativity, mathematics, and physical work. Using their own designs and measurements, carpenters may draw up plans for the addition of a house deck or building a home entertainment unit. Certainly simple geometry comes into play when fitting the pieces together to construct something, but carpenters often rely on a basic understanding of physics as well to know how structures can hold up different amounts of weight. This type of handiwork can be especially gratifying because you create a physical object that displays your craftsmanship.

Since many carpenters are self-employed, they must cultivate business skills in order to survive. They buy supplies, estimate costs, bill clients, and manage their own accounting. They often budget money for advertising and maintaining a truck. Those who are strong communicators can easily explain their services and work together with homeowners, small businesses, and local contractors to make their vision a reality.

Because they are frequently knowledgeable of the entire construction process, many carpenters ultimately advance to positions as carpentry

or construction supervisors. To rise to advanced positions, carpenters should be able to estimate the nature and quantity of materials needed to properly complete a job, and they must be able to accurately estimate how long a job should take to complete and what it will cost.

Opportunities are expected to be plentiful for at least the next 10 years, and although it has never been considered a glamorous career, TV home improvement shows like *Trading Spaces* and *Weekend Warriors* may change all that, making carpentry more popular than ever.

find your future cement mason

cement mason

At the foundation of all the world's most important structures—airports, highways, dams, and hospitals—is one basic ingredient: concrete. Concrete is a mixture of cement (a binding mix of calcium carbonate, silica, iron oxide, and alumina), rock, water, and sand. Cement can be poured and hardens with such strength that it provides a solid foundation for even the biggest of buildings. Whether buildings stand tall through the test of time and nature's elements often depends on the quality work of the cement masons and concrete finishers—some of the most important and sought-after members of today's building team.

Cement masons and concrete finishers pour concrete into its place to create foundations. They then level, smooth, and shape its surface. Masons prepare the site that concrete will be poured into. They measure the site (for example, the basement for a new clothing store), estimate the amount of cement that will be needed, and set a form that holds and properly aligns the concrete. Along with a team of laborers, masons use shovels and other tools to spread out poured concrete. Then, using a straightedge tool, they level it out (or "screed" it) until it is flat, and

Get Started Now!

Start mixing in learning and experiences that will help you become a mason:

- Take math, mechanical drawing, and science classes.
- See if there's a Habitat for Humanity building homes near you and volunteer, or contact a local concrete contractor to see about visiting a work site or working as a helper.
- Get acquainted with cement by purchasing a decorative garden stone kit at your local craft and hobby shop. In the process of making a useful keepsake (or gift for someone special), you'll be mixing and working with small amounts of cement.

Search It!
The National Concrete Masonry Association at **www.ncma.org** and Operative Plasterers and Cement Masons International Association at **www.opcmia.org**

Read It!
Concrete Products On-line at **http://concreteproducts.com** and CM News at **www.ncma.org/ periodicals/news.html**

Learn It!
- On-the-job training
- Two- to three-year apprenticeship program (including 144 hours of classroom instruction per year)

Earn It!
Median annual salary is $30,659, plus overtime.
(Source: U.S. Bureau of Labor Statistics)

Find It!
For more information on job possibilities, visit **www. masonry-training.com**.

Hire Yourself!

You've been hired as a cement mason to lay the foundation for a new house. Determine how much concrete will be needed for a 30-foot-long, 30-foot-wide, three-foot-deep concrete slab. You should be able to get the answer by either consulting with a local home improvement store or researching on-line or at the public library. Then write a plan for you and your team of laborers to complete the job and answer the questions: What tools will you need? What will you do if it becomes very windy? What work must be done to ensure that the concrete won't crack? What will you do if it does crack?

finally smooth over the surface with a tool called a bull float. Throughout the process, a mason must pay close attention to the weather and treat the concrete with chemicals, water, or covering (like burlap or plastic). Heat, wind, and cold can all affect how the concrete cures, or hardens.

Before the material hardens, a concrete finisher takes over. The finisher uses tools—such as edgers to make rounded edges, and groovers to create joints and grooves in the concrete—which help prevent concrete from cracking. The concrete is then re-troweled (spread and smoothed). Colored concrete or terrazzo (a floor covering made with marble or stone) may be added for decorative purposes. For surfaces that will remain exposed, like walls or ceilings, the finisher might remove loose concrete with a hammer and chisel and cover the whole area with a cement paste to give it a nice finish. Many cement masons also work as finishers, and vice versa.

Both jobs require spending a lot of time on your knees but pads help prevent injuries. They also help keep workers' skin away from chemicals in the concrete. Water-repellant work boots also give protection. Since work on wet concrete has to be finished in a short time frame once it is started, overtime is common.

Employers prefer to hire high school graduates with driver's licenses. Training consists of on-the-job lessons that may be part of a three-to-four year apprenticeship.

Work for masons and finishers is expected to be plentiful in the coming years as new structures like highways, subways, factories, and schools are built. Repair work on existing structures will also provide jobs. However, the amount of available work fluctuates with the seasons, as much of it is done outdoors and requires good weather.

find civil engineer future

civil engineer

The next time you ride over a bridge, or walk through the airport on your way to catch a flight, you have a civil engineer to thank for helping you on your way. Civil engineers design and oversee the building of public structures: roads, buildings, airports, tunnels, dams, bridges, and water supply systems— among other things.

In addition to the everyday buildings you see, civil engineers are also responsible for some of the world's greatest wonders and most notable technical achievements. Some of these include the Hoover Dam, the Brooklyn Bridge, and the Channel Tunnel (the "Chunnel"), which connects Britain to France.

Civil engineers have a reputation for being math and science geeks— but this is only half the picture. While they do toil away applying math and science theories to develop economical solutions to technical problems, they also make these things happen. Civil engineers must devise schedules, see that all parts and labor are accounted for, manage a budget, solve problems on-site, and make sure that what they are building

Search It!
The American Society of Civil Engineers at *www.asce.org*

Read It!
Civil engineering news at *www.cenews.com*

Learn It!
- A bachelor's degree in civil engineering needed for entry-level jobs; a master's to advance; a Ph.D. for research and university teaching
- Explore engineering programs at *www.abet.org* (Accredited Board for Engineering and Technology)

Earn It!
Median annual salary is $55,740. (Source: U.S. Department of Labor)

Find It!
Find job listings at *www.civilengineeringjobs.com*, or by checking out opportunities at big firms like Con Edison (*www.coned.com*) and government agencies like the Environmental Protection Agency (*www.epa.gov*).

Get Started Now!

Use these strategies to get ready for a future in civil engineering:

- Take as many math and science classes as you can, including plane geometry, physics, chemistry, geometry, trig, calculus, and computer science.
- Look into internships at local engineering firms.
- Study up on the marvels of modern civil engineering— read books on the world's greatest dams, bridges, tunnels, and parks, and gain an understanding of the planning, money, labor, design, and innovation that goes into each one.

Hire Yourself

The city of Detroit wants to build a bridge over the Detroit River. There are three bridge types from which they could choose: beam, arch, and suspension. Go to *http://science.howstuffworks.com/bridge.htm* and learn how each one works differently.

Now, do some research and find one example of each type. On poster board, write down the characteristics of each bridge: its location, the length it spans, the year it was completed, how long construction took, who designed it, and the manpower involved in its construction. Then decide for yourself which type you think Detroit needs!

"works." In short, they are not only responsible for designing a project, but for seeing it through as well.

Within civil engineering, there are many specialties. A few include environmental, transportation, urban, and water. For example, an environmental engineer can be the scientist who ensures a community has safe drinking water or minimal air pollution by building water treatment plants and air pollution control systems. One in transportation might build a railway system; an urban engineer might develop park plans for a city; and a water engineer constructs—you guessed it— things like pipelines and dams. One specialty does not necessarily exclude another, though. It's possible to be a Renaissance man—or woman—of civil engineering.

A civil engineer goes through three stages to complete a project. The first, preconstruction, is the planning stage. During preconstruction, the engineer must survey land, develop a timetable for the project, decide on a budget, and figure out how much material and how many workers he'll need. Surveying aside, most of this is "desk work."

The next stage is implementation. This is when actual building begins, and when the engineer really gets to know his crew of workers. He is on-site, making sure construction goes smoothly, and progress is being made. Civil engineers basically live on-site during this phase— sometimes for days at a time.

The final stage is infrastructure maintenance, and this occurs after the project is finished. During infrastructure maintenance, the engineer conducts tests to ensure that whatever has been built can withstand the amount of stress it is likely to encounter. It's the equivalent of shaking a thermos to make sure it doesn't leak. And when all is said and done, our civil engineer goes back to the office to file paperwork and start thinking about his next project. Some projects take years to complete!

Civil engineers have a variety of options when it comes to employers. Aside from typical engineering firms, they can work for government businesses, utility companies, or telecommunications companies, like Verizon, among others. Civil engineers can also set up their own consulting firms and work for themselves.

While only a bachelor's degree is required for entry-level jobs, some schools offer five-year programs to obtain both a bachelor's and a master's. Co-op programs let you earn a bachelor's while gaining on-the-job experience. A master's can set you on a faster track for advancement. But the education process for civil engineers doesn't stop there—they must continually keep up with technological advances.

As far as jobs are concerned, the outlook is good—with over 10,000 openings in the field of civil engineering in 2005 alone and more expected in the years ahead. For those interested in building structures that improve communities, now may be the time to consider a career in this field.

find construction your foreman future

Search It!
The Construction Management Association of America at *www.cmaanet.org*

Read It!
CM eJournal at *http://cmaanet. org/ejournal.php*

Learn It!
● Bachelor's degree in civil engineering, construction science, construction management preferred
● Experience as a construction craft worker (e.g., carpenter, mason, plumber)

Earn It!
Median annual salary is $63,500. (Source: U.S. Department of Labor)

Find It!
Construction managers can search for openings at big-name firms like McGraw-Hill Construction Dodge (*http://dodge.construction.com*, Turner Corporation (*www. turnerconstruction.com*), or by checking out industry sites like *http://cmaanet.org/ employment.php*.

construction foreman

As the boss of the construction job site, the foreman is the one who makes sure a project is completed on time and supervises the work crews. His or her biggest concern is making sure the craftspeople and laborers perform efficiently and skillfully. The foreman keeps careful track of their progress and makes sure duties are done on schedule. The general contractor may serve as a foreman but often the general contractor looks at the big picture of a construction project and the foreman handles the onsite minutiae. When and where will material be delivered? What equipment needs to be on site for the next day's activities? Who is scheduled to work?

From their broad base of construction knowledge and the ability to quickly read blueprints, foremen must know enough about all kinds of construction-related specialities to determine whether each job is being performed correctly. At times they may even have to showcase this knowledge by demonstrating how specific tasks are to be done.

Get Started Now!
Take charge of your future and start preparing for a career as a foreman:
● Look into management courses—in particular, courses dealing with human resources (since foremen deal with so many personnel issues).
● Build a strong background in mathematics and computer science.
● Try to watch a foreman in action. Call a local construction firm and see if you can interview a foreman and follow him or her during a day's work.

Hire Yourself!

Being a foreman means taking charge and being the boss. The first step is hiring the right people. To see if you're foreman material, a local home builder has asked you to write a list of the types of skilled construction craftspeople you would need to construct a home and a plan to establish whether or not they have the right skills for the job.

A foreman depends on workers to show up on time, work steadily, follow instructions, and produce quality work, and if they cannot do so, the foreman must be ready to replace them. These professionals are also cost-controllers—they will purchase supplies that match the budget constraints, and they will only employ skilled workers that the developer or owner can afford.

A foreman on a large project may oversee a particular area such as excavation and laying the foundation, erection of the structural framework (the floors, walls, and roofs), or the installation of the building systems (the electricity, plumbing, air-conditioning, and heating). They not only supervise a team of workers, but they have to work with engineers, architects, and other construction professionals to ensure that their designs and specifications are being followed.

This is outdoor work that involves directing a large number of people. Leadership skills are essential as workers have to respond to a foreman's decisions and respect his or her judgment. And in general, foremen have earned their position by having built up years of experience in the construction field. Many start out as construction laborers—plumbers, carpenters, masons, or electricians. With such extensive experience, a foreman can advance to become a construction company owner. Opportunities should increase especially for those who keep up with new technologies (electronics used to make "smart" buildings, construction laws and codes, energy efficiency, and environmentally friendly structures).

Search It!
The Construction Management Association of America at *www.cmaanet.org*

Read It!
CM eJournal at *http://cmaanet. org/ejournal.php*

Learn It!
- Bachelor's degree in civil engineering, construction science, or construction management preferred
- Experience as a construction craft worker (e.g., carpenter, mason, plumber)

Earn It!
Median annual salary is $63,500. (Source: U.S. Department of Labor)

Find It!
Construction managers can search for openings at big-name firms like McGraw-Hill Construction Dodge (*http://dodge.construction.com*), Turner Corporation (*www. turnerconstruction.com*), or by checking out industry sites like *http://cmaanet.org/ employment.php*.

find your future

construction

manager

What do you think would happen if your school had no principal and the teachers and students were responsible for running it? It probably wouldn't be pure chaos, but a lot of things would go wrong—or wouldn't happen at all. For instance, teachers would have no authority to go to with curriculum questions and they'd spend valuable time dealing with discipline issues—a job formerly for the principal and the administrative staff. If materials and resources (including other teachers!) were lacking, teachers would have to deal with this entirely on their own. In short, there would be no presiding force to pull things together. A construction manager is similar to a principal in this way: he or she plans and coordinates construction projects.

A construction manager (sometimes called "constructor," "construction superintendent," "general superintendent," and "project engineer," among other things) usually has no hand in the physical process of construction. Rather, once he or she is given the design for a project, the manager is responsible for hiring workers, including specialty trade contractors (such as plumbers and electricians), drawing up a schedule

Get Started Now!

Use these strategies to get ready for a future as a construction manager:
- Check out certification programs at the American Institute of Constructors at *www.constructorcertification.org*.
- Speak up in class! Volunteer to be a team leader in group projects.
- Math and science will come in handy as a good foundation for construction management/engineering study in college.

Hire Yourself

Your neighbor has signed you on to build a tree house in his backyard for his kids. Your job is to draw up a plan for the project. First, sketch a design of the shed and write down a list of all the things that need to be done and in what order (build floors, then walls, then add roof, etc.) Go to a home improvement site, such as *www.diynet.com* or *www.lowes.com*, and find out what materials you'll need, and what they'll cost. Then, decide how many workers you'll need and what tasks each worker will do. Use a calendar and draw up a schedule for when you'll be working and what should be accomplished on each day. Finally, calculate the total cost of the project.

and seeing that it is followed, acquiring and allocating the necessary resources (including special permits and licenses when necessary), and ensuring that the work is faithful to architectural drawings. The manager also works with cost estimators to figure the most economical way of getting the project done. Sometimes this involves using complex formulas and advanced computer software.

When there is a large-scale project, such as a strip mall or skyscraper, different methods of management are used. For instance, the owner can hire a general contractor, under which the construction manager works, or if a management firm handles the project, it can hire a construction manager who reports directly to the firm, rather than the owner. In a collaborative method called the design-build system, architects, general contractors, subcontractors, and owners all sit down at the table to map out the project's design. During this process the construction manager offers input on the design and may or may not head up construction when the design is finalized.

Construction managers spend a lot of time both inside and outside. They usually work out of either a main office or a field office that is on-site. And in case of emergency situations, such as a potentially damaging storm, they must be on-call around the clock. That's why they carry either a pager or a cell phone, and take their work with them wherever they go via laptop computers. Construction managers work long and bizarre hours, too. Projects will sometimes require workers to work morning to night, seven days a week, because of a time crunch. But the flip side of this is that there can be substantial breaks between different projects.

Large projects, as you might imagine, are not done in one fell swoop, under the management of one person. The construction of an expansive office building, for instance, would require land to be cleared, sewage systems installed, foundations laid, the interior (walls, roofs, counters, floors, and so on) built, and landscape detailed. Each phase may be put under the management of one contractor.

Meetings are another important component of the construction manager's job. They talk regularly with the craft workers, engineers, architects, owners, and vendors (individuals and firms from whom necessary materials are purchased). And if conflict arises, the construction manager must be prepared to mediate a fair solution. If, for example, the architect's design is not being carried out to to his or her exact specifications, the construction manager must communicate to the contractors, subcontractors, or craft workers how and why the work needs to be modified.

Construction managers may work for themselves, or they may work on a salary basis for contracting firms or for owners themselves. Employers generally prefer to hire those who have worked in the industry themselves either as construction workers or supervisors, and who have also received a bachelor's degree in a related field such as construction science or engineering. Although it's not always required, managers are starting to receive certification through organizations like the American Institute of Constructors (AIC) or the Construction Management Association of America (CMAA). Certification indicates to an employer that you are serious and qualified.

For those who excel in leadership positions and can juggle many responsibilities at once, construction management is a rewarding field that is expected to offer growing opportunities through 2012.

demolition engineer

It's rare to find a job where you get paid to destroy things. But demolition engineers get to do just that—knocking over structures with heavy equipment, bulldozing dilapidated buildings, even blowing up skyscrapers and stadiums with explosives. Although demolition can look like destruction and chaos, there are very particular methods for knocking down buildings in a safe, efficient manner and disposing of the debris.

When a building is deemed unsafe or outdated and has to be removed to make way for a newer structure, demolition experts are called in. Types of demolition vary from job to job. The crane and wrecking ball may first come to mind, but sometimes concrete elements are cut and removed piece by piece to minimize dust, noise, and damage. To break materials apart, advanced tools such as water jets and thermic lances, which use intense heat, may be used. Another method is called pressure bursting, which can require hydraulic machinery to break apart materials. Other tools include demolition hammers, chipping hammers, pavement breakers, and diamond wire saws. On smaller jobs—breaking through a wall perhaps—workers will swing a sledgehammer.

Get Started Now!

There is no crash course in demolition, but you can get started on a career path:

- Visit a demolition site and get a first-hand look at heavy equipment such as bulldozers and cranes. Try to read up on the capabilities of heavy equipment on-line, in catalogs, and at the library.
- Get experience working at a construction site and specifically look into part-time opportunities with a demolition contractor.

Search It!
National Association of Demolition Contractors at *www.demolitionassociation.com* and the International Society of Explosives Engineers at *www.isee.org*

Read It!
Demolition Magazine at **www.demolitionmagazine.com**

Learn It!
- High school diploma
- On-the-job training
- Some vocational and trade schools offer courses in demolition

Earn It!
Annual salary ranges between $50,000 and $150,000. (Source: National Association of Demolition Contractors)

Find It!
Check listings of demolition contractors at *www.concretenetwork.com/concrete/demolition/contacts*.

Hire Yourself!

We Destroy Buildings, Inc. knows that safety is the number one concern for the demolition business. They've hired you to make a list of safety precautions they must take during any major demolition project. Your list should include ways to protect people, nearby structures, and the environment. Try to list at least 10 safety measures.

When a building is too big to dismantle with heavy machinery, demolition experts may cover a building with up to 1,000 pounds of explosives and set off what is called an electrical implosion. The explosives go off in the middle of the building first and then spread to the outer walls, which makes the building collapse in on itself. Just the right amount has to be used or damage can be caused to power lines, underground sewer tunnels, and neighboring buildings.

Before any blasting begins, a contractor writes a blasting survey, which includes transportation, storage, and inventory of explosives, as well as fire precautions. An engineering survey is performed to decide if there were any chemical, gases, explosives, or flammable materials on site. Contractors have to make detailed plans for removing toxic materials such as asbestos or lead.

Careful preparations must always be made to ensure the safety of workers on the job and in the vicinity of the demolition. Clearly, the entire area must be marked for authorized personnel only. Safety equipment on hand includes respirators, hearing protection, safety nets, lifelines, fall protection, warning signs, and eye and face protection. Contractors must also have a plan for emergencies, if there's an unexpected fire or medical crisis.

After the blast, contractors must wait a set amount of time to let dust, smoke, and fumes subside before workers can go into the site and start the process of removing the debris, usually by the truckload to a landfill or incinerator. Finally, they conduct a post-inspection to make sure no hazardous material is left behind.

Instead of demolishing, some contractors will deconstruct, which involves taking apart a building piece by piece. When dismantled, a contractor can use recyclable materials, including bricks, concrete, lumber, electrical sockets, and steel. For deconstruction, workers come in with hammers and crowbars; they pull up floors, unhinge doors, take cabinets off walls, and unscrew light fixtures. Then they sort through the pieces and salvage what they can. (Find out more through the Institute for Local Self-Reliance at *www.ilsr.org*).

Organization, leadership, management, and a broad base of construction skills are key to getting this job done. Because so many components are involved in a demolition project—from safety issues to labor management to deadlines—contractors have to deal with a lot of pressure. Contractors are also expected to be the experts on government regulations, so they must learn all the standards and protocols that are enforced by the Occupational Safety and Health Administration.

Because it really is such involved work, there is a great demand for good demolition contractors, and every time a job is completed, the demolition expert has helped in construction progress, making way for the next generation of building.

drafter

Search It!

Association for Computer Aided Design in Architecture at **www.acadia.org**

Read It!

CADD Primer at **www. caddprimer.com**

Learn It!

Most CADD professionals learn by attending programs at technical institutes, community colleges, and some four-year colleges and universities.

Earn It!

Median annual salary is $37,330. (Source: U.S. Bureau of Labor Statistics)

Find It!

Most drafters work for architectural or other firms. Look for job leads with the American Design Drafting Association (**www.adda.org**).

drafter

Like any successful endeavor, constructing a building takes lots of planning. Before construction even starts, a drafter analyzes building codes, designs room arrangements, draws up blueprints, and calculates how many supplies will be needed. Drafters once did all of their work manually, using pencils, pens, compasses, protractors, and other tools at a drawing board. Now, computer-aided design and drafting (CADD) programs have replaced many of these tools. Drafters trained to use CADD programs are called CADD professionals or operators.

CADD professionals apply computer programs to make detailed technical drawings and plans that construction crews read to create buildings. These drawings must be accurate down to the tiniest detail, with specific information on dimensions, necessary supplies, and technical features. Rather than set up intricate models to test building designs and materials, CADD simulates how a building will look and function before workers lay down a single brick. With a few clicks of a mouse, CADD programs can reuse design pieces in buildings with a similar style or automate standard parts present in certain building types, like kitchens in restaurants. These programs can store information on local building codes and laws, or help determine what types of materials will work best in certain designs. After the drafter finalizes a

Get Started Now!

To design your career as a drafter, start now by doing the following:

- Take courses in mathematics, computer science, and drafting.
- Practice drawing can be helpful. Carry around a sketchpad and draw as many buildings as you can. It will give you a basic sense of building structure.

Hire Yourself!

You are constructing a new gym for your local community center with a racquetball court measuring 20 feet by 20 feet. Each wooden board that makes up the floor is 1 foot by 5 feet and costs $12. Before construction begins, the chief architect wants to know how many boards to purchase and how much the total cost will be. Sketch out the best way to complete the project and make an estimate of the anticipated cost.

building's plan, CADD can also calculate a materials list to help figure out the final cost of a project.

Basic math skills are important in creating and understanding CADD drawings, and artistic skill helps CADD operators plan attractive buildings. Good communication and interpersonal skills help CADD professionals communicate their design to other members of the construction crew. Computer literacy helps students pick up CADD software quickly. Most operators learn how to use CADD through programs at technical schools or community colleges, but CADD classes are also a part of many drafting programs at four-year universities. Because new CADD programs spring up periodically, professional design and drafting organizations frequently sponsor continuing education classes for members.

CADD professionals have one of the most comfortable jobs in the construction industry, spending most days in front of computer terminals in air-conditioned offices. However, some CADD operators act as an architect's representative, making frequent trips to the construction site. About half of all CADD professionals work at architectural firms. However, knowing how to use various CADD programs can help you get a job drawing plans for highways, bridges, electrical wiring, or even cars or airplanes. Because many firms hire several CADD professionals, operators can move up the corporate ladder by managing their department or team.

Search It!
The National Electrical Contractors Association at *www.necanet.org*

Read It!
Electrical Trade News at *www. necanet.org/pressroom/ releases*

Learn It!
Completion of a three- to five-year apprenticeship program is required.

Earn It!
Median annual salary is $41,392. (Source: U.S. Department of Labor)

Find It!
Electricians may be self-employed but many work for construction contractors. Check out employment leads at *www.necanet.org*.

find your electrician future

electrician

Watching television. Surfing the Web. Talking on the phone. Microwaving a bag of popcorn. What do all these things have in common? They would not be possible without electricity—which is why the job of the electrician is so important. Without them to harness the power of electricity, we would never be able to do many of the activities that we usually take for granted.

Electricians have the job of installing and maintaining electrical wiring systems that serve a broad range of purposes, some of which include climate control (heating, air conditioning), telecommunication (phone, Internet), and general electric (lighting, appliances, etc.). They may install systems for homes, businesses, and factories alike, or work in some sort of manufacturing capacity. They also do maintenance work to ensure these systems are working properly.

Electricians follow blueprints to locate where they should install circuits, panel boards, load centers, and outlets. A circuit is the tube or piping that contains electrical wiring, and is usually installed behind a partition, such as a wall. Load centers and panel boards are both used to control light, heat, or power circuits, and are also installed "out of the way." This may mean they are placed in a cabinet or cutout box, and against the wall, accessible only from the front. If you've ever had to

Get Started Now!

Use these strategies to prepare for a career as an electrician:
- High school classes in math, shop, and graphic design will come in handy.
- Hobby shops and toy stores sell kits that help young people experiment with electricity and learn basic principles.
- Check out The National Joint Apprenticeship Training Committee (NJATC) at *www.njatc.org* to learn about apprenticeship programs.

Hire Yourself!

You've been hired to rewire a six-room house. Draw a rough blueprint that details the layout of all the rooms in the house. Go to *http://science.howstuffworks.com/power.htm*. How many outlets would be reasonable for each room to have? Where would circuit breakers and wiring be located? Fill in all this information on the rough blueprint that you draw.

flip the switch in the fuse box, then you should be familiar with load centers and panel boards!

Electricians then connect the wiring they've installed to circuit breakers and transformers. Then they use instruments such as ohmmeters, voltmeters, and oscilloscopes to test the wiring. Those probably sound like weapons in a sci-fi movie, but they are simply methods of measuring electricity. An ohm is a measure of electrical resistance, a volt is a measure of electro-motive force, and an oscilloscope is simply a device that displays the changes in electrical current.

Although most electricians perform some degree of maintenance work, some specialize in it. They may return to homes, for instance, to rewire systems, or replace an old fuse box, in order to preempt a breakdown. When breakdowns do occur, however, electricians must be available to fix the problem as soon as possible. You don't know what you have until you lose it—and electricity is no exception! Countless daily and nightly activities depend on electricity, so although electricians usually work standard 40-hour weeks, those in maintenance often have to work odd hours at night and on weekends. Electricity is very powerful and potentially dangerous, so electricians must be extra cautious with all their work.

Most electricians learn the trade by completing a comprehensive apprenticeship program that lasts three to five years and qualifies them both to install and maintain electrical systems. Most programs combine approximately 144 hours of classroom instruction with 2,000 hours of on-the-job training each year. Going this route, electricians may work either in construction or as full-time maintenance technicians. Electricians must also be familiar with the National Electrical Code, and usually have to pass a test on the code before going to work.

The job outlook for electricians is bright: By 2012, the current number of jobs is expected to increase by 21 to 35 percent. If you are an able-bodied person with a desire to bring power to your community, then a career as an electrician just may be the one for you.

find your future
environmental engineer

Search It!

The American Academy of Environmental Engineers at *www.aaee.net*

Read It!

Pollution Engineering at *www.pollutionengineering.com*

Learn It!

- A bachelor's degree in civil, chemical, mechanical, or environmental engineering
- Master's or Ph.D. necessary to advance
- Schools offering environmental engineering degrees are listed at *www.enviroeducation.com*

Earn It!

Median annual salary is $61,410. (Source: U.S. Bureau of Labor Statistics)

Find It!

To check out entry-level engineering jobs, visit *www.engcen.com/entry.htm*.

environmental engineer

In the movies, superheroes often save the earth by destroying an alien spaceship, changing the path of an enormous asteroid, or ridding the world of man-eating zombies. In real life, the task of protecting our planet and the health of its inhabitants falls to a different type of superhero: the environmental engineer.

Environmental engineers show clients such as factory owners and construction firms how to limit and correct the damage they may cause to nature. Since they are very knowledgeable of pollution laws maintained by the federal Environmental Protection Agency, engineers also help companies meet these government regulations. Making sure pollution levels are within legal limits requires testing the water, air, and soil on a site to measure for toxins.

Their work may involve helping build newer, environmentally friendly businesses or helping improve older businesses. Once problems

Get Started Now!

Start preparing for a career in environmental engineering now.

- Take science and math classes, especially biology, chemistry, physics, algebra, trigonometry, and geometry. Also, be sure to develop your computer skills.
- Familiarize yourself with the problems facing the environment. See if you can volunteer at your town or county's recycling center, or join an organization dedicated to helping the environment. Sierra Club has a great website that tracks environmental issues by state at *www.sierraclub.org*.

Hire Yourself!

You are creating a plan to help your school create less waste. Write a two-page proposal that includes details for implementing several of the following ideas (or some of your own): starting a cafeteria program to recycle aluminum, glass, and plastic; starting a school compost heap; arranging for leftover food to be donated to a homeless shelter; organizing a school grounds cleanup; encouraging the school board to invest in recycled paper products.

are identified, engineers then create plans to minimize or eliminate pollutants. They may design sewer and purification systems to keep the water clean; they may build safe ways to dispose of toxic waste.

On a larger scale, these engineers devise plans to fend off such Earth-threatening enemies as global warming, acid rain, and ozone depletion. For example, in the automobile industry, environmental engineers have pushed for the use of more water-based paints, which produce far fewer pollutants than oil-based paints. In San Francisco, they've helped to introduce wind and solar power as a clean, alternative energy source. And in New York City, new "Don't Walk" signs were installed that use far less energy than their predecessors.

Most environmental engineers specialize in one specific area. Specialties include hazardous waste management (dealing with toxic chemicals that are a byproduct of industry), protection against nuclear radiation releases, and public health (organized efforts to protect, promote, and restore public health).

These professionals spend plenty of time outside, inspecting work sites and collecting samples to be tested later, but the job requires a lot of desk work as well. Engineers write up the results of their research, recommend ways to correct problems, and draw designs for operations that will reduce pollutants. To assist in their analysis, they increasingly use computer technology, such as Geographic Information Systems (GIS), which use photos taken from airplanes and satellites to investigate an area of land, and computers that track the movement of waste through water.

Before signing up for this career, be ready to do some serious studying. Candidates should have excellent math skills and expertise in a variety of sciences, including biology, chemistry, and physics. They should also enjoy working with others to solve complex problems. A good environmental engineer will also think "outside of the box" to find innovative solutions for today's environmental problems.

Demand for these professionals is increasing so much that there are currently not enough skilled professionals to fill all available positions. Engineers may work for the government or for private industries (including architecture, surveying, and research). As the earth's population continues to grow, so do the amount of toxins caused by modern life. That's why the environmental engineer's efforts to protect the planet are more important than ever.

find your future
equipment manager

equipment manager

In some ways, equipment management is like a car rental service. Equipment managers maintain a fleet of vehicles that are available for different uses. Instead of cars, the vehicles are all heavy equipment—graders, bulldozers, scrapers, cranes, lifting equipment, concrete and asphalt, loaders, and dump trucks. An equipment manager may rent them out to different contractors and developers for various projects, or they may maintain a fleet for one particular construction company or a city or state department of transportation or highway division.

Managers maintain their vehicles either by having a team of technicians on staff to make repairs and check them over, or by outsourcing this type of work to independent repair technicians. If vehicles are beyond fixing, managers must purchase new ones.

The majority of an equipment manager's job involves tracking and keeping records. All the maintenance and repairs must be recorded. Equipment will be assigned to different work sites, and the manager must know where the vehicles are at all times. Managers figure out how to move these large pieces of equipment from one site to another. Sometimes they send technicians to deliver and retrieve equipment. When equipment is done being used for a particular job, the manager

Get Started Now!

Want to be the master of the big construction machines? Here's how to start:

- Read about heavy equipment and visit a construction site to get a firsthand look at bulldozers, backhoes, cranes, and more.
- Take accounting and math courses to be ready for all of the financial work that goes into management.

Search It!
Association of Equipment Manufacturers at **www.aem.org**

Read It!
Up & Running at **www. equipment.org/uprun.htm**

Learn It!
- Training and experience as a mechanic
- On-the-job training

Earn It!
Median annual salary is $45,000. (Source: CollegeGrad.Salary.com)

Find It!
Opportunities can come through major construction firms as well as heavy equipment manufacturers, such as Caterpillar (**www. caterpillar.com**) and John Deere (**www.johndeere.com**).

Hire Yourself!

A construction company wants you to help them shop for new equipment. Go to the websites of the manufacturers that make these big machines—Caterpillar (*www.caterpillar.com*) and John Deere (*www.johndeere.com*), for example. See if you can find pricing information and descriptions of two major pieces of equipment, such as a truck, crane, backhoe, or bulldozer. Compare the prices and features of similar equipment. Make a chart or poster as a way to report your findings to your client.

will note how much fuel has been used and, in the case of a truck for example, they will mark down mileage (just like at a car rental service).

Schedules are important to track a technician's work hours, monitor progress, and assign when repairs are to be made. Managers must be able to define a worker's tasks for the day, spelling out objectives that can be reached within realistic timeframes. To make sure mechanics can repair vehicles quickly, managers may maintain a storage area for parts. They keep a detailed inventory of what's been used and what needs to be ordered.

The cash flow is another item for the tracking list. Managers keep a keen eye on hours billed by workers and costs for parts and new equipment. They carefully review all invoices for errors. To make their job easier, much of the scheduling and tracking has been computerized.

Although there is no set educational path, many equipment managers start as equipment technicians and learn all the ins and outs of repairing these big machines. But to master this job, they need some solid math skills. Following the finances requires some basic accounting skills, and billing can sometimes involve formulas based on "machine hours" and distances traveled.

Advancing at this job means improving efficiency. New technologies have helped. Some fleet managers who dispatch delivery and service vehicles can keep in contact with users through new wireless communication systems. Some managers investigate the use of new fuels and methods to reduce engine wear—all of which can keep their vehicles up and running.

find your estimator future

estimator You decide to make dinner for the family, so you go to the grocery store to purchase a few items. You only have $20, but you figure that it should be enough. At check-out, however, your total comes to just over $26. You have estimated incorrectly, and are forced to put back a few items—which is a bit embarrassing, but no big deal. Cost estimators, on the other hand, face a bigger dilemma if they make a mistake. They are responsible for projecting how much a construction or manufacturing endeavor (such as a building or a new product) will cost. And if they miscalculate, a company could end up losing a lot of money.

Cost estimators must look at all the factors that will ultimately determine how much a project costs. This means they must consider

Get Started Now!

These strategies may help you on your way to becoming a cost estimator:

- Practice your estimation skills—anything helps! You could run for treasurer of a school club, or even for the entire class. This will give you the chance to work with teachers and other students to estimate the costs of organizing a dance, printing the yearbook, or staging a school play.
- Statistics and other math classes will help; estimating involves the use of a lot of formulas. English classes will hone your writing skills for all those reports!
- Read about cost estimator certification at **www.sceaonline. net/content.asp?contentid=109**.
- Contact a member of the public works department, and find out how much a recent project in your community cost. (This is taxpayer money, so it should be public information and cost breakdowns may be available on the Web.)

Search It!
The Association for the Advancement of Cost Engineering at **www.aacei.org**

Read It!
The Construction Financial Management Association (CFMA) news feed at **www.cfma.org/ newsfeed.asp**

Learn It!
- A bachelor's degree in construction science, engineering, or related field
- Well-rounded experience in the construction industry

Earn It!
Median annual salary is $47,550. (Source: U.S. Department of Labor)

Find It!
Search for jobs through the Society of Cost Estimating and Analysis at **www.sceaonline.net**; with major firms like Marshall & Swift at **www.marshallswift.com/ career_opps.asp**; or through construction companies like McGraw-Hill at **www.construction.com/ CareerCenter/default.asp**.

Hire Yourself!

You have been hired by a state university to estimate the cost of building a new student center, complete with a movie theater, food court, music practice rooms, and study halls. But first (since you have experience as an architect as well!) you are going to construct a model of the building, based on an existing one. Compile a list of materials you'll need, such as balsa wood or modeling glue. Estimate the amount of each material you'll need, and how much each will cost. Then complete a cost summary. Follow up at a site like *www.ehobbies.com*. How close was your estimate?

the individual costs of parts, labor, location, and machinery (anything from crane rentals to computer software). They must also take into account potential set-backs and be prepared to pay for delays due to inclement weather, accidents, shortages of materials, or other unforeseen obstacles.

Cost estimators can work in either manufacturing or construction. Those working on construction projects begin with the bid submission. Estimators review plans and study blueprints, and then visit the site of the project in question. He or she must investigate how accessible the site is, how plentiful necessary resources such as water and electricity are, and how the nature of the site will influence the building process: is it level? Will it drain well? Will it be necessary to remove many impediments, such as rocks and trees? All this information is included in a report that will become one component of the entire estimate for the project or the bid.

After the site visit is completed, the estimator gets to work on the quantity survey, or takeoff. It is at this point that precision comes into play and the number-crunching begins—or "takes off." This is almost exactly what it sounds like: during this process, the estimator evaluates how many units of each resource (number of ceiling tiles or two-by-fours, for instance) will be needed, and how much each individual unit will cost. Standard estimating forms must be completed with this information. While the estimator prepares his or her own list of costs for goods and services, he or she also analyzes the estimates that subcontractors submit. In the case of large-scale projects, there may be several estimators specializing in different things: one may focus on electric costs, while another determines the cost of glass or siding.

Sizing up labor costs is the next step in the estimating process. After quantity surveys are completed, the cost estimator prepares a cost summary that also includes labor, overhead (insurance, taxes—things that are not physically part of the construction process, per se), and markup of construction materials, among other miscellaneous expenses.

Since they deal with endless cost comparisons and calculations, estimators are very much like accountants and above all else they need to excel at crunching numbers. Fortunately, computer programs are there to help calculate costs. Writing and organizational skills also come in handy when preparing reports.

Employers prefer hiring estimators with substantial experience in the industry, so those with some education in construction have an advantage. To demonstrate competency, many estimators take college courses that prepare them for certification. As opportunities in this field are expected to grow through 2012, those with a talent for numbers and a fascination with building may find a career in cost esti-

Search It!
Visit the Floor Covering Installation Contractors Association at *www.fcica.com* and the National Tile Contractors Association at *www.tile-assn.com*

Read It!
Read *Bottom Line e-News* at *www.fcica.com*

Learn It!
● A high school diploma is necessary
● On-the-job training is the norm
● Three- to four-year apprenticeship programs, combining on-the-job training and classroom work, are available

Earn It!
Median annual salary is $32,593. (Source: U.S. Bureau of Labor Statistics)

Find It!
Check the International Union of Painters and Allied Trades at *www.iupat.org/jobcorps/index.html*.

flooring mechanic

In every house, you can pretty much count on a few things: walls, ceilings, and floors. And whether that floor is tile, carpet, wood, or whatever else, without a flooring mechanic, you may as well be living in a tent.

Flooring mechanics, also known as installers and finishers, are responsible for installing the indoor flooring in homes, offices, and virtually anywhere inside. Most mechanics are trained to install a particular type of floor.

A carpet installer's job may look simple, but there is a lot more to installing carpet than meets the eye. First, they must correct any imperfections in the surface that is to be covered by the carpeting (such as lumps on the concrete) so that there is no chance of the imperfections showing through the carpet. Then, they must carefully measure the room so that no carpeting is wasted. This is where you put all those geometry principles that you learned to work! Carpet installers use a series of tools, such as a power stretcher to stretch out the carpet. Even though your bedroom might look like it's covered by one large piece of carpet, it's actually several pieces that are joined together by a special

Get Started Now!
● Build basic math skills—flooring mechanics have to measure rooms and materials. Shop classes can help hone hands-on skills.
● Visit home improvement centers and read through home improvement catalogs to get an idea of how diverse floor coverings can be.
● When it comes time to buy a new rug for your home, dorm, or bedroom, do the work yourself. Measure the area to be covered and think what style and material will best suit the space.

Hire Yourself!

You've been hired to tile a room that is 10 feet wide and 25 feet long. The tile the customer selected is a 10-inch square. Assuming 1 inch between tiles, draw a diagram to show how many tiles will be needed, and how they will be laid out.

tape that is activated by heat. Carpet installers also use hammers, drills, staple guns, and glue to make sure their carpet stays put.

A floor installer, on the other hand, uses similar tools to lay down such material as vinyl, linoleum, rubber, or cork. These materials are used mainly for decorative or soundproofing purposes, or to be easier on the feet (shock-absorbing). Oftentimes, floor installers nail or staple a layer of wood in between the floor and the material. This helps protect the material from wear and tear.

Tile setters and marble setters install tile and marble, respectively, to walls, ceilings, and roofs, as well as to floors. Unlike carpet layers, tile setters must first make sure that the floor is completely level. They lay out the tiles before affixing them to the floors—then use cement mortar to keep the tiles in place. The joints between the tiles are then filled with grout, a very fine cement.

Floor sanders and finishers smooth wooden floors with floor-sanders. They also remove glue from in between the pieces of wood using a knife or wood chisel. Then, they finish the wood with coats of varnish or oil.

Flooring mechanics tend to be self-employed or work for flooring contractors. A high school diploma is usually required. Unlike many other construction workers, flooring mechanics work mostly indoors. They must be willing to spend a lot of time bending and working on their knees.

Job availability is often good, especially as older buildings need refurbishing. However, because wood is now available pre-finished, jobs for wood floor finishers are not as plentiful. Carpet installers have the most opportunities at this time.

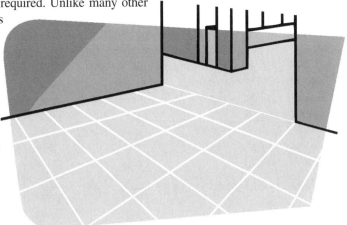

Search It!
The Associated General
Contractors of America at
www.agc.org

Read It!
AGC Smart Brief at ***www.***
smartbrief.com

Learn It!
● Bachelor's degree in business,
  or construction-related field
● Several years' experience in
  construction industry

Earn It!
Annual salary range is $40,000 to
$250,000.
(Source: Contractorzone.com)

Find It!
General contractors are self-
employed and obtain jobs by bid-
ding for projects. Contractors
usually join the local chapter of an
industry organization such as the
Associated General Contractors
(***www.agc.org***) to find out about
construction projects.

general contractor

Have you ever walked by a construction site, and seen a sign that read something like "Smith, Smith & Smith, General Contractor"? A contracting company, or a general contractor, is near the top of the construction hierarchy—right below the owner or developer of a project. Once the general contractor's company wins a construction bid and signs a contract to do the work, he or she becomes the most authoritative "go-to" person on that project. The successful completion of a project rests on the contractor's shoulders.

Contractors get work by submitting bids stating how much they will charge to do a specific job. To find these jobs, they look for advertisements on-line or in journals, or simply hear of projects through networking. The developers who place the ads will award the contract after comparing bids, services offered, the reputation of the contractors, and other factors.

The general (or prime) contractor, also known as a GC, is the party that contracts for the construction of an entire building or project. GCs

Get Started Now!

Use these strategies to pursue a career as a general contractor:

● Recommended high school classes include math, shop, and drafting. Any architectural, engineering, and business classes will also come in handy.
● Leadership skills are essential for contractors, so take advantage of any opportunities to build them—by being captain of a team, leader of a band, or editor of a paper.
● Some construction firms offer internships. Hands-on training never hurts!
● Check out ***www.contractors-license.org*** for state licensing information.

Hire Yourself!

You've been hired to build a house. First, jot down all the components a house needs: plumbing, heating, air conditioning, driveway, landscaping, roofing, masonry, etc. Devise a preliminary schedule for the building process. Include start and end dates for subcontractors to finish their work. When you are finished, try going to this site: *www.b4ubuild.com/resources*. Compare schedules. How reasonable were your estimates?

can work on their own or as part and head of a company, coordinating and directing the activities of all the laborers on the project. Sometimes, for smaller projects, GCs may use only their own resources or workers. For larger projects, however, the GC is responsible for hiring subcontractors to perform specialty tasks including installation of heating, electrical wiring, plumbing, demolition, masonry, roofing, and landscaping. When a project demands the coordination of several of these specialties, developers usually know it's in their best interest to involve a general contractor.

Like the name suggests, general contractors have extensive experience. They are "generally" knowledgeable in all or most of the above specialty tasks. They know which government permits and licenses they'll need to obtain before beginning and who to speak to concerning construction and redevelopment in a given city or county. Since they are established in the field, licensed GCs have worked in various capacities: they know not only which subcontractors are needed to complete the job, but which ones have a reputation for reliability, and are thus more likely to get the job done well, in a timely manner. Planning is central to the contracting business. The GC's job basically is centered on good planning: he or she plans when subcontractors should arrive, on what schedule they should complete their individual tasks, what materials will be needed and when they will be needed, when inspections should be performed, and what paperwork needs to be filled out. All of this requires numerous on-site meetings and countless phone calls. It is not uncommon for a GC to be working on several projects simultaneously. The payoff for most GCs is earning a percentage of the total final cost of a project, so their annual earnings can be substantial depending on how many projects they complete.

In addition to considerable industry experience, a general contractor must also possess substantial business insurance, such as workman's compensation and liability. The GC accepts all responsibility for a

project—be it responsibility for completing the job on time, or responsibility for on-the-job mishaps and injuries. If the customer cannot offer a similar deal in the way of insurance, subcontractors make them compensate for it in added fees.

Since construction projects are becoming increasingly complex, employment opportunities for general contractors are expected to grow. The state of the economy, though, is always hard to predict, and improvement or development projects are usually more prevalent in a good economy. But if you have the mind for taking a plan and "building" a reality out of it, then you might consider general contractor among your career options.

find your future glazier

glazier

Think about the number of times a day you come in contact with glass. From the mirror in your bedroom to the skylight at the mall, to the door on the frozen food section at the supermarket, glass is everywhere. It's the glazier's job to cut, install, and replace glass in these settings as well as a variety of construction environments. Construction companies, architectural firms, and glass shops all employ glaziers.

Residential glazing involves installing mirrors, shower doors, and windows, while big commercial projects often require installing security windows or even glass panels on skyscrapers, sometimes using aluminum and steel to reinforce the glass. Glaziers may also install and replace glass windows in storefronts, from supermarkets to auto dealerships to banks.

While the glass is often cut before it arrives at the construction site, sometimes a glazier must cut the material working with a straightedge as a guide and a special glass cutting wheel. Today, many glaziers use computers that help them make more precise cuts. If the glass is very heavy, cranes are used to lift the pieces, holding the glass firmly with large suction cups. Once glaziers position the glass in place, they must secure it

Search It!
The National Glass Association at **www.glass.org** and Glass Association of North America at **www.glasswebsite.com**

Read It!
U.S. Glass Magazine at **www.usglassmag.com**

Learn It!
- High school diploma or GED
- On-the-job training
- A three- to four-year apprenticeship (consisting of on-the-job training and 144 hours of classroom instruction or home study per year)

Earn It!
Median annual salary is $30,128. (Source: Payscale.com)

Find It!
To find information on employment opportunities, visit the Employment Center at the National Glass Association website at **www.glass.org**.

Get Started Now!
See your way to a career as a glazier.
- Glaziers often start as helpers, cleaning up broken glass and helping out at glass shops. Find a shop in your area to see if they are looking for helpers.
- Glass layouts are often done on a computer. Being proficient with a computer can help you land a job.
- Take a course in blueprint reading or mechanical drawing.
- You may be able to find a local glassblower in your neighborhood who gives lessons. Classes like these can introduce you to the properties of glass.

Hire Yourself!

You've been hired to cut and install the glass on a wall of a new building. Your boss wants 25 equal-sized glass panels to fit neatly into the wall. First you have to create a model. Use a standard 11-by-17-inch ledger-size piece of paper positioned horizontally as the model for your wall. Then take several pieces of construction paper and decide how to cut the paper into panels that will represent glass windows. Use glue or tape to secure your paper "windows."

using putty, mastic, or other paste-like cement, or by using bolts, rubber gaskets, glazing compound, metal clips, or metal or wood moldings.

Glaziers can learn their work solely on the job or complete a three- to four-year apprenticeship that combines on-the-job-training with classroom instruction. To certify their competency, glaziers can take a series of proficiency tests. A glazier's job can be dangerous and uncomfortable at times, doing a lot of bending and lifting and working on scaffolding at great heights. They must also handle power tools such as saws, drills, cutters, and grinders—not to mention tons of glass. An essential part of a glazier's training involves learning to work safely with the equipment and materials involved with glasswork.

Glaziers are expected to be in demand in the near future, especially as many buildings install new glass systems. For example, shatterproof glass that can withstand explosions and bulletproof and smash-proof glass have become very popular. Energy efficient windows that hold in heat help lower heating bills for homes and businesses. With these types of technological advancements, glaziers can make home and business improvements that can potentially save money—and lives!

find
heating, ventilating, and air-conditioning
your technician future

heating, ventilating, and air-conditioning technician

You work in Georgia, and it's the middle of July. With the humidity, the heat index is 101°F. You're sitting in your office but you aren't sweating the slightest bit. In fact, you're quite comfortable. Why? Because you're inside and the air conditioner is on full blast. A heating, ventilating, and air-conditioning (HVAC) technician has thankfully brought you the gift of cool air.

HVAC technicians build, install, and repair systems that control temperature, humidity, and air quality. Usually they specialize in either providing heat or cooling. Some technicians deal exclusively with air-conditioning and refrigeration equipment, installing pipes, motors, compressors, and condensing units. Others focus strictly on installing furnaces powered by oil, gas electricity, or solid fuels (wood and coal,

Get Started Now!
Use these strategies to get ready for a future as an HVAC technician:
- If metal shop is offered at your school, take it.
- Shop, math, chemistry, applied physics, mechanical drawing, blueprint reading, and computer classes provide the perfect academic foundation.
- Check out resources and programs sponsored by national heating and cooling associations, such as this one: **www.phccweb.org/foundation/career.cfm**.

Search It!
Air Conditioning Contractors of America at **www.acca.org** and Plumbing-Heating-Cooling Contractors–National Association at **www.phccweb.org**

Read It!
HVAC industry news at **www. hvacnews.com**

Learn It!
Six-month to two-year programs in heating and air-conditioning at junior or community colleges are suggested, along with on-the-job training.

Earn It!
Median annual salary is $35,000. (Source: U.S. Bureau of Labor Statistics)

Find It!
HVAC technicians can search for work by region at sites like **www. hvaccareers.com**, or by visiting large climate-control manufacturers like Rheem at **www.rheemac. com** or Trane at **www.trane. com**.

Hire Yourself

Space that an air conditioner is equipped to cool is measured in British Thermal Units, or BTUs. About 30 BTUs are required to cool one square foot. Go to *www.home.howstuffworks.com/ac4.htm* for a more in-depth explanation. Different air conditioners are made for different-sized spaces. Research four different air conditioners and find their "cool capacity," and determine the square footage of spaces for which they would work. Where might you see each? What type of air conditioner would be best for cooling your classroom and your bedroom? Compile a short list.

for example). They put in pipes, pumps, and water lines, as well as ducts and vents through which the air passes. Following blueprints or design specifications, HVAC technicians perform their jobs using hammers, metal snips, drills, pipe cutters and benders, measurement gauges, and acetylene torches. The job involves a lot of hands-on tool work, to say the least.

Both heating and cooling experts have concerns about air quality. Furnace installers run tests after installation to check for carbon dioxide and oxygen levels. Air-conditioning and refrigeration technicians must be sensitive to the release of refrigerants, specifically hydrochlorofluorocarbons (HCFCs) and chlorofluorocarbons (CFCs). If not vented into the proper cylinders, CFCs and HCFCs contribute to the depletion of the earth's ozone layer. With this concern for conserving, recycling, and recovering harmful substances, HVAC technicians are partially environmentalists and protectors of the planet.

During the off-season of a furnace or air-conditioning unit (summer and winter, respectively), technicians may return to do maintenance work. While air-conditioning mechanics may return only if the system is not working properly, heating equipment technicians do routine calls to check up on the units. This involves cleaning and replacing filters and ducts—which become a breeding ground for impurities during winter.

As with other construction jobs, this is gritty work that can demand long hours. Temperatures can fluctuate from very hot to very cold, and when people lose their heating or air conditioning, repairs need to be done immediately. In addition to the dangers of handling some heavy equipment, technicians must take precautions with hazardous refrigerants, fuels, and other substances.

Although some HVAC technicians still receive only on-the-job training, attending technical school or enrolling in an apprenticeship program puts you one step ahead of the game. Technical schools can usually be completed in two years, apprenticeship programs in three to five. Apprenticeships are typically run by local chapters of professional construction associations, such as the Plumbing-Heating-Cooling Contractors–National Association. Subjects covered include the theory and design of heating and ventilation systems, blueprint reading, and the fundamentals of installation and upkeep. In addition, technicians working with refrigerants are required to pass a written exam to ensure they can handle them properly.

"Out with the old, in with the new" certainly applies in the world of heating and cooling systems. As more and more cost-efficient, energy-saving technology is being developed, the job outlook for HVAC technicians is very good with positions expected to increase by up to 35 percent over the next 10 years.

Search It!
The International Union of
Operating Engineers at
www.iuoe.org

Read It!
Past and recent articles from the
International Operating Engineer
magazine at ***www.iuoe.org/
OE%20newspaper/magarch.
htm*** and excerpts from *Practicing
Planner* at ***www.planning.org/
practicingplanner/default1.htm***

Learn It!
- A high school diploma is usually
  required
- On-the-job training or an apprenticeship program are the norm

Earn It!
Median annual salary is $35,235.
(Source: U.S. Bureau of Labor
Statistics)

Find It!
For information on apprenticeships
and training programs, visit ***www.
iuoe.org/training/job_corps.asp***.

**find your future
heavy equipment operator**

heavy equipment operator

Bulldozers, piledrivers, and cranes—
the monster machines of the construction world—move the heavy loads
and manipulate large volumes of material that mere human hands cannot. And it's up to the heavy equipment operator to harness the power
of these mechanical beasts of burden.

Heavy equipment operators are responsible for operating several different types of construction equipment. Bulldozers and similar
machines called excavators are used to smooth out the earth, or remove
and dump dirt, tree branches, and rock. These machines are essential in
prepping a job site. Operators working on this type of equipment might
also operate cranes and forklifts, used to raise materials like steel and
wood into the air.

Another type of equipment operator works to pave roads. A tamping
machine, for example, vibrates thousands of times a minute to pound
material into the ground. Asphalt paving machine operators regulate the
temperature of hot asphalt by turning a set of valves. They also control
the flow of asphalt onto the road. Similarly, concrete paving machine
operators control the release of concrete.

Get Started Now!
- Equipment operators need to be in good physical shape.
  Strength and balance are particularly important.
- Contact a construction company and ask if they will give
  you a tour of a machine like a bulldozer. Ask for an expla-
  nation of the different controls in the machine.
- Newer heavy equipment is often equipped with electron-
  ic controls. Basic electronics or computer skills can help.

Hire Yourself!

A trade school is beginning to make a simple manual about heavy equipment. The company would like you to write a brief report about any of the following types of construction equipment: bulldozer, grader, tamping machine, asphalt paving machine, or pile driver. Use the Internet or local library to find information, including how a worker operates it. Make sure to include a diagram of the equipment.

Other heavy equipment operators work piledrivers—machines that drive beams of wood or steel into the ground to support buildings or other structures, like bridges.

Heavy equipment operators are often responsible not only for operating their equipment, but maintaining it and making sure all of its parts work. They must also pay close attention to safety instructions, as the machines they are working on pose a potential danger because of their size and complicated controls.

A heavy equipment operator works almost entirely outdoors in almost any weather. They should be in good health and have good hand/eye/foot coordination, as many types of machines often require the operator to use combinations of foot pedals, levers, switches, and dials all at once. A good sense of balance is also important, as the equipment can bump and jerk.

Job opportunities are expected to be good over the next several years for heavy equipment operators, although work tends to slow when the weather gets too cold. In addition to new construction, repair work on existing construction, especially roads and highways, will fuel the creation of jobs.

While many operators learn their work on the job, there are other options. Apprenticeships involve on-the-job training and 144 hours a year of classroom instruction for three years. Since you will learn to use more than one type of machine during an apprenticeship, you may have a better chance of landing a good job. Additionally, some trade schools offer their own training programs.

The heavy equipment operator is a vital part of a construction crew. Sitting atop a perch high above the ground, they hold in their hands the awesome power of working machines that have made construction the booming industry that it is today.

Search It!
American Road and Transportation Builders Association at *www.artba.org*

Read It!
Transportation Builder magazine at **www.artba.org/transportation_builder/tb_index.htm**

Learn It!
- High school diploma encouraged
- On-the-job training

Earn It!
Median annual salary is $28,400. (Source: American's Career InfoNet)

Find It!
Cities, counties, and state departments of transportation employ many highway workers. Also check highway contractors listed at *www.artba.org*.

find your future — highway maintenance worker

highway maintenance worker

Next time you go for a drive, keep your eye on the road. It's always good safety advice, but this time, really look at the roads you're driving on. They represent millions of long hours and back-aching work—all performed by our nation's highway workers. Whether in the city, country, or suburbs, roadways connect us together and without them we'd all have a hard time getting to work, vacationing, and visiting friends.

Highway workers patch broken and eroded pavement, filling potholes for instance. They dump and tamp asphalt and other bituminous material like tar, using a pneumatic tamper. To spread material and smooth the material, they rely on the rake, and to apply the final oil to the surface they operate special sprayers. To make the roads safer, highway laborers fix guardrails and markers and paint fresh yellow and white dividing lines.

A large portion of their work is not on the road at all but on the side of the road or on the islands between roadways. Here, they may take on the role of landscaper, helping to clear brush, mow grass, weed, and plant flowers and trees. They may also unclog drainage and remove obstruc-

Get Started Now!
Prepare for a career in highway maintenance:
- Learn some practical math (ratios, proportions, and conversions).
- Look into part-time job listings with your state department of transportation. A summer working on highways can help you decide if this is the right work for you.

Hire Yourself!

Your state has started a campaign to reduce traffic fatal-
ities. Part of the effort is to make the highways safer
by repairing them. Drive a few miles on a highway,
thruway, or parkway near you and write a list of specific
things that could be done to improve that stretch of road.
Prepare a field report to submit to your state department of
transportation.

tions from ditches, catch basins, and culverts. Sometimes they use heavy
equipment to remove rockslides from the shoulder. Other off-road duties
include picking up trash and scattering pest control poisons. Most of
these workers need a license to drive the large trucks that transport workers and equipment and sometimes weigh as much as three tons.

Highway workers must be in prime physical shape and ready to work
outdoors in the bright sun and around busy traffic. (The traffic can be a
real hazard—the ARTBA reports that one
highway worker is killed on the job every
three days.) These laborers are comfortable
with using manual and power tools, as well
as heavy equipment, such as steamrollers,
tractors, and snow plows. Basic math
knowledge is helpful (for measuring
amounts of asphalt and paint needed, for
example), as well as the ability to work as
part of a team.

On the professional end of this spectrum
are the highway and civil engineers who
plan and design highways, bridges, and
other types of transportation systems. These
positions require at least a bachelor's degree
in engineering.

There is expected to be average growth
for all types of highway construction positions. As long as automobiles remain our
prime means of transportation, opportunities to work on our country's roadways will
continue to grow.

Read It!
ISdesigNET at **www.
isdesignet.com**

Learn It!
- Bachelor's or associate's degree
  in interior design
- The Foundation for Interior
  Design Education Research
  (**www.fider.org**) accredits
  two- to five-year professional
  programs

Earn It!
Median annual salary is $39,180.
(Source: U.S. Bureau of Labor
Statistics)

Find It!
Check out job opportunities at
www.InteriorDesignJobs.com.

find interior designer your future

interior designer

In the construction business, interior design is like the icing on the cake. After the foundations are laid, walls are built, roofs are secured, and the entire physical structure is completed, the interior designer steps in to add the beauty while keeping practical considerations in mind. They design interior spaces in private homes, public buildings, business offices, restaurants, stores, hospitals, hotels, and theaters and make them attractive and useful.

When you're in a space that's both comfortable and useful, you may not even realize all the elements that have come together to make it enjoyable. With artistic elements of color, light, scale, and balance in mind, the designer—with input from the client—decides on furnishings, light fixtures, and finishing touches like color, rugs, and decorations.

Drawing on a broad knowledge of paints and wallpaper, as well as woods and textiles, designers plan the colors and textures for the walls. They pick fabrics for window curtains that will complement the overall

Get Started Now!
Create a career in interior design:
- Attend a home and garden trade show. Interior designers usually exhibit at these shows, which are typically held at civic centers in major metropolitan areas.
- Television shows about interior design, such as *Trading Spaces*, are more popular than ever. Watch them regularly and you will learn from the experts.
- Go to major home improvement stores and study the supplies that line the shelves.
- Work on a home improvement project with your parents or family, or simply begin by figuring out ways to improve your bedroom.

Hire Yourself!

A hip new magazine for young people knows that you have style. They want you to present a basic design for the ultimate young-adult bedroom. When you draw your plan, show where all furnishing would be placed and write down specifics about floor coverings, wall colors, window curtains, etc. Use pictures from magazines or websites, fabric samples, and paint chips from a paint or hardware store to illustrate your ideas.

color of the room. For the floors, they suggest different approaches, from putting down shag throw rugs to leaving wooden parquet floors exposed. By reviewing blueprints, designers can plan to scale how furnishings will be arranged. These can include sofas, chairs, dining room tables, stereo equipment, a television, lamps, and works of art. Interiors can be simulated on computers using the latest design technology, and designers can easily show clients how rooms will look and make changes to the plans with a few clicks of a mouse. They will also bring samples of paint and upholstery to get their client's opinions.

People skills are extremely important for designers because clients are very sensitive when it comes to how their living and work spaces should be arranged. That's why designers share plans with clients every step of the way. Designers may also work closely with architects and a construction crew, recommending specific fixtures (track lighting in the ceiling, for example, or built-in bookshelves and cabinets). An interior designer's plans may be incorporated at different stages of the construction process—at the beginning or end of a new building project or when it's time to renovate an older room or structure.

Interior designers often specialize—some will focus strictly on homes while others will be experts at business design. Some zero in even further and design only restaurants or bathrooms or kitchens. Functionality is always a concern and it may be even more so in a business, such as a restaurant that not only needs a comfortable dining area but work stations and a kitchen.

Although much of their time is spent planning, many professionals get hands-on in supervising the work of painters, drape installers, or carpet layers. Some designers work for specialized design services or retail furniture stores, but many are self-employed, so they must know the basic principles of running their own business. It's important that they are well-informed about safety issues and government building codes that can affect their designs. Along with creativity and artistic sensibility, math skills are also needed for measuring and planning how a space will be arranged. Because the career has become so sophisticated, today's designers typically have a degree in interior design.

As construction projects continue, interior designers are finding more work, and an increase of the elderly population has recently spurred new opportunities with the building of more institutions, facilities, and planned communities.

find your ironworker future

ironworker

Your office is on the 55th floor—except, it isn't an office yet, and there isn't any floor. You're an ironworker, and it's your job to construct the skeletons of skyscrapers, bridges, stadiums, and more using steel girders, columns, and other construction materials. (Note: Even though the primary metal used is steel, these pros are known as ironworkers.)

While many of these skilled workers live life on the edge, literally balancing on narrow beams many stories above the ground, others work on terra firma. Ironworkers called assemblers and fabricators actually make the structural metal (such as iron, steel, or aluminum) used on construction sites. At the site, structural ironworkers (who assemble the structures) may unload the materials and use devices like cranes and forklifts to move them into position. Then, steel beams, girders, and other material are bolted and welded together to form the skeleton of the final product. Reinforcing ironworkers create steel bars called rebar and place them in concrete. This helps reinforce concrete structures and prevents them from collapsing. Structural and reinforcing ironworkers often work outside, at times in bad weather. They must be in top physical shape, with good eyesight and balance. The work can be dangerous, but safety training and

Search It!
The International Association of Bridge, Structural, Ornamental and Reinforcing Iron Workers at *www.ironworkers.org*

Read It!
Select articles from *Ironworker* magazine can be read at *www.instituteiw.org*

Learn It!
A typical requirement is a three- to four-year apprenticeship that includes classroom and shop instruction.

Earn It!
Median annual salary is $40,700. (Source: U.S. Bureau of Labor Statistics)

Find It!
Commercial and industrial construction companies recruit ironworkers. Apprentice programs can be found by contacting your local ironworker union (*www.ironworkers.org/locals/localdisplay.php*).

Get Started Now!
Iron out a path to a career as an ironworker:
- Learn basic construction skills. Many hardware stores offer clinics; you can also read books and visit websites to learn about construction to become familiar with the tools of the trade.
- Look on-line or in the yellow pages for local construction companies. Ask if you can visit a work site to see what being an ironworker is all about.
- Take math, mechanical drawing, and shop classes.

Hire Yourself!

Imagine that you are a seasoned ironworker with years of experience. You've been invited to talk to your son or daughter's class about your work. Use Internet resources like those you'll find at *www.howstuffworks.com* to create an amazing poster illustrating how steel is made.

precautions help reduce the risk of injury. They follow a strict set of standards to ensure that a structure is assembled properly.

Ornamental ironworkers install building elements such as window frames and elevator shafts after a building has been completed. They make sure that each piece is fitted properly, then weld or bolt it to the rest of the structure.

Teamwork is essential for ironworkers. Some will unload and prepare steel so it can be easily hoisted. Other workers attach cables that a crane will use to move material. Another worker may guide the crane operator while another works the crane.

Ironworkers almost always start out as apprentices working with local union representatives. On the job, apprentices get hands-on practice unloading materials, welding, and rigging materials to a crane. In the classroom, they study the basics of erecting, rigging, welding, reinforcing, and blueprint reading. With time and experience, they can work their way up the ladder to a supervisory position. In fact, a large percentage of construction company presidents and contractors started out as apprentices.

Although many fabricating jobs have shifted out of the country, ironworkers have remained in demand as new construction projects continue and repair work is required on older structures.

find your future
landscape architect

Search It!
The American Society of Landscape Architects at *www.asla.org*

Read It!
The Dirt, landscape architecture news digest, at *www.asla.org/land/dirt.html*

Learn It!
- Bachelor's degree in landscape architecture required; master's preferred
- For a list of accredited colleges visit *www.asla.org/nonmembers/accredited_programs.cfm*

Earn It!
Median annual salary is $47,400. (Source: U.S. Bureau of Labor Statistics)

Find It!
Find out about current opportunities at the ASLA website (*www.asla.org/nonmembers/joblink.cfm*), or at a commercial design firm such as LandDesign (*www.landdesign.com/green/index.html*).

landscape architect

Think about a park in your area. How are the trees, walkways, flowers, and bushes situated? The way these elements come together to make a park more attractive and practical is the work of the landscape architect. His or her job is to design outdoor spaces, for public or private use, so that natural and manmade elements (such as roads and buildings) come together in an artistic and pleasing way. You can find their work in playgrounds, college campuses, shopping centers, golf courses, parkways, industrial parks, and residential developments.

Landscape architects usually arrive on the scene before a project even begins. Whether that project is an airport or a strip mall, they start by working with surveyors, architects, and contractors to help develop a plan for the site. This team of workers will decide how roads and buildings will be arranged. Then, the landscape architect will often get together with environmental scientists and foresters to consider how resources

Get Started Now!
Pave the way for a career as a landscape architect:
- Take botany or horticulture classes offered at your school or local community college.
- For all those reports and designs you'll be drawing up, you will need to be computer-savvy. Take whatever classes in design, desktop publishing, and word processing you can.
- Visit a botanical garden or park near you and take note how beauty and practicality are combined.
- To read about obtaining a landscape architect license, visit the Council of Landscape Architectural Registration Boards at *www.clarb.org*.

Hire Yourself!

The county just bought a plot of land to build a new park, and you've been hired to design the landscape! To get design ideas, visit another local park or, if you'd rather, go on-line and research a famous one—like Central Park in New York City, or Lincoln Park in Chicago. Take notes on all aspects of the park: walkways, bike paths, shrubbery, flowers, trees, skate ramps, and facilities. Then, make a detailed sketch of your park that includes all the basic components from the parking lot to playground to the garden to the outdoor stage to any other features that you want to include.

might be preserved. The next step for the landscape architect is to construct a detailed plan for new or modified topography and vegetation, as well as decorative attributes. For instance, if a lake will become part of the landscape, or rows of evergreens will border a parking lot, then these will be included in the plan. Much like regular architects, landscape architects create detailed visuals using computer-assisted design (CAD). Sometimes, they also make miniature 3-D models.

When the landscape design is being formulated, several factors have to be taken into account. What is the budget? What is the purpose of the project? How much land is available? What is the climate? How is the soil? How is storm drainage and how will the site be affected by forces both natural and manmade? Landscape architects must also keep themselves informed of any local, state, and federal regulations—such as zoning regulations and laws protecting certain animals and wildlife regions such as wetlands.

Once the preliminary plan is finished, a landscape architect will draw up a proposal for the client. This may include photos of vegetation or topography that is similar to the area being developed, drawings, models, cost estimates, and land-use studies. Then, when the go-ahead on the proposal is given, the landscape architect will design a more extensive layout that includes everything—where elements will be situated and how they will be constructed. So, for a landscape architect to be successful, he or she needs to be something of a pragmatic artist, able to arrange the components of a site in a way that is both functional and pleasing to the eye.

While some landscape architects try their hand at many different projects, others specialize in one type of landscaping, such as residential projects, parks, highways, or office buildings. Others work with environmentalists on conservation projects, such as preserving forests or beaches. Still others are involved in "traffic-calming" projects, which aim to mitigate congestion by modifying roads and their surroundings. Others work with homeowners to create functional and beautiful landscapes and gardens.

To get your foot in the door, a bachelor's degree in landscape architecture is the bare minimum education required and a master's degree is often recommended. Once you are out of school, you most likely will have to pay your dues by working as an "apprentice" or "intern landscape architect" until completing a rigorous licensing process.

For those who have an eye for aesthetics and like the idea of bringing together beauty and function, now may be an ideal time to pursue this career. According to the Bureau of Labor Statistics, opportunities are expected to grow by as much as 35 percent by 2012.

find mechanical your engineer future

Search It!
The American Society of Mechanical Engineers at *www. asme.org*

Read It!
Mechanical Engineering magazine at *www.memagazine.org*

Learn It!
This highly technical field requires at least a bachelor's degree, typically in mechanical engineering, and preferably a master's.

Earn It!
Median annual salary is $62,880. (Source: U.S. Bureau of Labor Statistics)

Find It:
Visit ASME's Tools of Discovery Career Information at *www.asme. org/education/precollege/discovery/carmast.htm* or *www. mechanicalengineer.com*.

mechanical engineer

What do engines, robots, home appliances, elevators, and escalators all have in common? They're all designed and built with the help of a mechanical engineer. Their talents apply to such a wide range of projects that mechanical engineers are often called the general practitioners of engineering. Aircraft, bicycles, a building's ventilation system, and even an artificial heart are products of mechanical engineering. Almost anything you can think of as a machine started off in the mind of a mechanical engineer, and the common factor among all these is moving parts.

Get Started Now!

- Four years of math and four years of science in high school is the usual requirement for acceptance into a good engineering program. Take classes in computer science, algebra, geometry, trigonometry, and calculus. Science— including biology, chemistry, and physics—is also important. Mechanical drawing can also give you an edge.
- Consider getting involved in an engineering competition, like FIRST, a national robotics contest. For more information, see *www.usfirst.org/robotics*. For a fun example of robotics in action, visit *www.asme.org/education/precollege/whyknot/index.htm* and see a machine that can continually tie and untie neckties.
- Many colleges offer degrees in mechanical engineering and their websites provide a valuable glimpse into the subject.
- Learn more on a variety of engineering topics at *www. howstuffworks.com*.

Hire Yourself!

You are a mechanical engineer working for a large construction equipment manufacturing company trying to increase the fuel efficiency of their heavy equipment vehicles. Investigate vehicles powered by alternative fuel sources (such as gas/electric hybrid cars, solar powered cars, and vehicles that can operate on vegetable oil) and write a report on how current vehicles might be rebuilt to accommodate these changes.

Since it is such a broad discipline, almost all mechanical engineers specialize in a particular area. Engineers may concentrate on energy systems, for example, studying how it is made, stored, and moved. They may work for a gas and electric company, coming up with new equipment to help deliver heat and air conditioning throughout homes. And as Americans become more concerned with the depletion of natural resources like oil, mechanical engineers are working on ways to harness energy from renewable sources such as sun and wind. Recently, skyrocketing fuel costs have convinced motor vehicle manufacturers such as Ford to invest money in developing more environmentally friendly cars.

Engineers who specialize in manufacturing create machines that improve existing technology. For example, they might invent a series of automated assembly line machines to put together a specific type of toy or fill hundreds of cans of soup in an hour. This type of engineer is careful to design machinery that will be efficient, environmentally sound, and easy to operate. They also work with robotics—much of the welding on new cars now is done by robotic arms.

Mechanical engineers rely on creativity and scientific know-how to improve today's everyday machines (like kitchen appliances) and invent the technology of the future. A mechanical engineer might envision a vacuum with amazing suction power or a piece of spaceship equipment that keeps astronauts safer. In the emerging field of biotechnology, mechanical engineers are working with doctors and biologists to create amazingly life-like artificial limbs. Within each specialty, roles are even more defined—mechanical engineers may work exclusively in research and development or manufacturing or maintenance or sales.

To become a mechanical engineer, you'll need at least a bachelor's degree, but many hold a master's. Your education often depends on your specialty—for example, if you want to work in aviation, you'll have to study fluid dynamics, or how both liquids and gases flow. Since engineering programs are very competitive, you'll need good grades in high

school. Excellent science, math, and computer skills are essential. Additionally, since so many aspects of the career involve teamwork, you must be able to work well with others.

As the needs of our society continue to change, so does the career outlook for a mechanical engineer. Though the number of manufacturing jobs available has decreased slightly, newer areas such as biotechnology and nanotechnology (involving the use of particles smaller than the eye can see) are leading to new and cutting-edge opportunities.

No matter what their expertise, mechanical engineers make our everyday lives easier and more convenient.

find your future

painter

Search It!
The International Union of Painters and Allied Trades at *www.ibpat.org*, Painting and Decorating Contractors of America at *www.pdca.org*, and National Paint and Coatings Association at *www.paint.org*

painter

When it comes to a construction job, the painter is the player on the team who comes in near the end and adds the finishing colorful touch. But a painter's job is not merely to make a building look good both inside and outside. Paint (and other sealers) can actually protect a building from wear and tear caused by weather and the environment.

Before the manual labor begins, the painter's first task is to choose the paint. There are many different types of paint. Some are oil-based, some are water-based. Some are mainly used outside, some inside. Working with the customer, the painter can choose the right paint for their project. For example, gloss paint cleans easily, so it is good for high-traffic indoor areas. Flat paint is good for exterior surfaces like vinyl and aluminum siding that may be dented, because flat paint hides imperfections well.

Before painting can begin, the painter must prepare the surface. This sometimes requires removing old paint (using techniques including sanding, wetting, and wire brushing) and always involves cleaning the walls and repairing any holes or cracks. For a new surface, a primer or

Read It!
Painters and Allied Trades Journal at *www.ibpat.org/about/journal.html*

Learn It!
● High school diploma and on-the-job training is the norm
● Some apprenticeship programs, combining on-the-job training and classroom work, are available

Earn It!
Median annual salary is $31,657. (Source: U.S. Bureau of Labor Statistics)

Find It!
Find job possibilities at the International Union of Painters and Allied Trades website (*www.iupat.org/jobcorps/index.html*).

Get Started Now!
● Basic math is helpful in determining how much paint is needed. It also comes into play when mixing paint colors.
● Get experience with paint and color on a small scale—paint models, woodwork projects, or even create your own paintings.
● A lot of young people find part-time opportunities painting—try to land a temporary painting job to see if you like the work.
● Color sense is also important. Play around with watercolors, oil paints, or a color wheel to see how different combinations can be made.

Hire Yourself!

You've been hired to paint the living room of an old house. Write a short essay describing what tools you'll need and what steps to take to ensure success, including meeting with the customer, planning a schedule, and prepping the surface. Also visit the paint department of a local hardware store and pick out paint chips or color samples that you think would be good colors for a living room.

sealer is typically applied. To get just the right shade for the customer, these skilled workers know how to mix colors. Some have a keen artistic sense, knowing exactly what tints will suit a particular room. Others rely on paint manufacturer's carefully calibrated paint formulas to get the tint just right.

Finally, it's time to paint. Depending on the surface and paint type used, the painter chooses from a variety of brushes, rollers, and even sprayers to apply a coat. For example, latex-based paints are best put on with a polyester brush, while a natural hog-hair brush absorbs the liquid too quickly. Rollers are often best for a large area; sprayers can cover a big space in less time but they can waste paint.

At times, painters work in high areas, especially if they are painting a tall building or a room with high ceilings. They may even work from scaffolding that is suspended with ropes or cables. Endurance is a vital quality for the job since painters stand most of the day, moving their arms in a repetitive manner, often stretching them over their heads.

Job opportunities for painters are expected to grow steadily in the near future. Even when new construction is at a standstill, there is often plenty of work re-painting older buildings. As there is little room for advancement, many painters do not stay with the job for many years, but this creates openings for beginners. A similar career choice is that of a paperhanger. Paperhangers paint, but also apply wall coverings such as wallpaper or fabric.

You don't have to be the next Picasso or Michelangelo to make an impact with paint. Whether a simple coat of white on an old dilapidated house, a deep purple on a master bedroom wall, or a sleek silver on the town's hottest new nightclub, paint makes our walls—and our lives—a little more colorful.

find plasterer and drywall installer your future

plasterer and drywall installer

Plasterers could be considered the smooth operators of the construction biz. When interior walls and ceilings are completed, plasterers step in to smooth over the rough cinder blocks and concrete surfaces using durable cement plasters, polymer-based acrylic finishes, and stucco. In some ways, they are construction's cosmetic surgeons, while painters and wallpaper hangers are the make-up artists.

A typical job begins by spreading a brown coat of gypsum-based plaster followed by a white coat of lime-based plaster. If the surface is wire mesh (called lath), a primary base or scratch coat is first applied. They finish the job with a mixture of lime, portland cement, and water. To get the end result of a smooth, dry, durable finish, plasterers rely on just a few fundamental tools—a trowel, a brush, some water, and a special tool called a *hawk* (a metal sheet with a handle underneath used to hold plaster, mortar, or other compounds). Occasionally, they will use

Search It!
Association of Wall and Ceiling Industries International (AWCI) at *www.awci.org*

Read It!
AWCI's *Construction Directions* at *www.awci.org/cd.shtml*

Learn It!
Plasterers learn the trade on the job through apprenticeships and other training programs. Some attend trade or technical schools.

Earn It!
Median annual salary is $33,092. (Source: U.S. Bureau of Labor Statistics)

Find It!
AWCI lists some of the major companies associated with plastering at *www.awci.org/buyersguide*.

Get Started Now!

Get a headstart on a wall-to-wall career by doing the following:

- General mathematics, mechanical drawing, and shop classes can lay the foundation for this career.
- Blueprint reading is often required, so any opportunities to learn this skill will help.
- Make a model out of papier-mâché to get accustomed to working with plaster of paris.
- Check with local construction firms and contractors for part-time work.

Hire Yourself!

A local modern art museum is redoing their walls with plaster. They want to feature a repetitive design in the plaster as a trim near the ceiling. Your job is to present five different types of designs, either drawn on paper or etched in your own plaster of plaster of paris or papier-mâché mixture.

plaster-mixing machines, power tools, and straightedges. Their handiwork helps make a room fireproof and soundproof as well. Exterior work can get heavier as these craftsmen apply a mixture of cement and sand (stucco) over concrete or masonry. For a decorative touch, the plasterer may add in small stones.

Most jobs, however, are completed indoors, so plasterers generally don't work under harsh outdoor conditions. But like so many construction jobs, stamina and balance are essential for climbing up ladders, holding materials, and applying the plaster to hard-to-reach areas. Some wear masks to filter out the dust that often gets in the air, and many leave a day's work looking ghostly with clothes stained white from plaster. These laborers can benefit from an artistic eye to create the smooth and sometimes decorative surfaces. Some even use plaster to cast ornamental designs. To learn the craft, those starting out typically train through apprenticeships or on-the-job programs.

Cheaper to install than plaster is drywall, which is a thin layer of gypsum between two heavy layers of paper. Where plasterers work fast with thick wet mixtures, drywall professionals work with panels that they must measure, cut, and fit, sometimes to accommodate windows, doorways, electrical outlets, light fixtures, air-conditioning units, and plumbing. Installers screw, nail, or glue the panels to hold them in place. Specialists called tapers often fill the joints between panels with a joint compound. They press a paper tape into the seams to smooth the imperfections. Another related career is the ceiling tile installer or acoustical carpenter who places acoustical tiles, blocks, strips, or sheets in ceilings or walls to help reduce sound or simply to decorate.

For plasterers, opportunities may be most abundant in Florida, California, and the Southwest, where exterior plaster work is most popular. Jobs for drywall installers may be even more plentiful than those for plasterers, but both fields are expected to grow in the immediate future. Plus, this field can be a great stepping stone to advance into bricklaying, supervising, contracting, or estimating.

find your plumber future

plumber

You've probably seen commercials on TV for liquid drain cleaner—the stuff that unclogs the gook stuck in a sink drain: old food, stray hair, etc. These cleaners are so good, the commercials say, that you'll never need a plumber again.

The commercials are wrong!

Difficult clogs still often require the handiwork of a trained plumber who may run a snake (a long flexible rod) deep into the pipes or use a plunger. Plumbing repairs, installation, and upgrades all require the help of a plumber.

When it comes to repairs, plumbers may have to fix leaks as well, tightening and mending joints. But they are also responsible for installing piping systems. They put water, waste disposal, drainage, and gas systems in new buildings and connect appliances such as bathtubs, toilets, water heaters, and showers to the piping. To connect these fixtures and make plumbing pipes fit together correctly, plumbers use special saws, cutters, benders, and soldering torches.

These skilled workers need to rely on both physical and mental "strength." They must be able to read blueprints to decide where piping needs to be laid, and build around such plumbing roadblocks as electrical systems and walls. Additionally, they must be able to lift heavy pipes, stand for long periods of time, and be willing to work in cramped conditions, under sinks and in crawl spaces. They're key players on a

Get Started Now!
- Take a shop class in high school. Math, especially some basic physics, is helpful. If possible, learn how to read blueprints.
- Find a local plumber. Ask if you can accompany him or her on a job to experience plumbing hands-on.
- Apply for a part-time job at a hardware store where you can learn about the instruments used by plumbers.

Search It!
The Plumbing-Heating-Cooling Contractors–National Association at **www.phccweb.org**

Read It!
Plumbing & Mechanical magazine online at **www.pmmag.com**

Learn It!
- A high school diploma or GED is necessary
- Four- to five-year apprenticeship with 144 hours of classroom instruction per year
- Armed forces training can count towards an apprenticeship

Earn It!
Median annual salary is $40,165. (Source: U.S. Bureau of Labor Statistics)

Find It!
Organizations offering apprenticeships can be found at **http://12.4. 18.10/index.htm**. Also, many plumbing opportunities are listed at the Mechanical, Electrical, Plumbing at Work website (**www. mepatwork.com**).

Hire Yourself!

A plumber is thinking of hiring you as an assistant, but he wants someone with at least a basic grasp of plumbing. He's asked all the candidates for the job to submit a simple diagram of a toilet and explain how it works. To draw your diagram and write a simple explanation, you'll need to do some research at your local library or bookstore (check out *The Complete Guide to Home Plumbing*), or go on-line and visit a site such as *www. howstuffworks.com*.

construction team but they often work alone, especially when called on to do repairs.

Plumbers belong to a category of workers that also includes pipelayers, steamfitters, and pipefitters. It's a pipelayer's job to lay concrete, clay, plastic, and cast-iron pipe for drains, sewers, water mains, and oil or gas lines. A pipefitter, on the other hand, installs and repairs pipe systems used in manufacturing, the generation of electricity, and to heat and cool buildings. A steamfitter installs pipe that moves gas and liquids and sprinklerfitters put in automatic fire sprinkler systems. Some may provide specialized piping for pharmaceutical and computer-chip manufacturers.

While some simply learn on the job, most plumbers begin their careers as apprentices. As they become skilled in the trade and the techniques for running a business, many become managers or owners of their own plumbing business. Demand for plumbers is expected to exceed supply over the next several years, so the job outlook is good as is the pay.

find
preservationist
your
future

preservationist

If you wanted to find a career that's the polar opposite of demolition engineer, it would have to be preservationist. Instead of tearing down old buildings, the preservationist restores and maintains old structures, including historical sites. Preservation architects plan how to stop or remove decay and prevent any further damage to buildings. They figure out how to best restore structures while maintaining their original character. Sometimes they will suggest ways to modernize, renovate, and convert buildings without ruining their historical integrity.

Also known as architectural conservators and heritage specialists, preservationists work to keep history intact in the form of old homes, log cabins, mansions, barns, farmhouses, churches, factories, museums, railway stations, and other structures. These buildings tell us about a society's lifestyle, culture, religion, construction methods, ethnic origins, economy, and other traits.

To do the job, preservationists start by analyzing the condition of a structure, taking notes, measuring, and taking photographs. Sometimes they test and evaluate the original materials for decay and durability. To

Search It!
National Preservation Institute at
www.npi.org

Read It!
Preservation Architect at *www. aia.org/hrc/newsletter*

Learn It!
- Many preservationists have a degree in architecture; others have an advanced education in historic preservation or architectural history
- Visit the National Council for Preservation Education website at *www.uvm.edu/histpres/ ncpe*

Earn It!
Median annual salary is $56,620. (Source: U.S. Bureau of Labor Statistics)

Find It!
Look for employment opportunities at *www.preservationweb.com*.

Get Started Now!

Those wanting to keep history alive can start by doing the following:

- Go on-line and read more about preservation. View samples of preservation work at *www.preservationweb.com*.
- Take courses in physics, chemistry, geology, geography, mathematics, social studies, and drafting.
- Check for summer job opportunities at local historic sites where you may get a taste of what restoration is really like.

Hire Yourself!

The president has declared your bedroom a national landmark! It's unclear exactly how this happened, but your job is to write a list of all the elements that preservationists will want to make sure are maintained in the years to come. Make a list of those architectural elements, from the paint to the light fixtures. For fun, add on a list of belongings that should be preserved in the room that capture this time of your life (for example, particular posters, CDs, etc.).

make sure repairs will maintain historical accuracy, preservationists become researchers, digging into records that tell how a building was constructed and from what materials. They comb through original drawings, documents, and maintenance records.

Once a general plan is in place for what needs to be done, preservationists may take up the role of a general contractor, overseeing the project from start to finish, including schedules and budgets. They will hire skilled artisans and tradespeople who can restore old structures, such as stained glass experts, ornamental statue specialists, and light fixture restorers. They may also know specialists who apply chemicals or other treatments that can stop decay or preserve materials.

Preservationists may work for local, state, or federal government offices, as well as private foundations and private homeowners—many of whom own homes that are designated landmarks. Those who contract preservationists count on them to know about local landmark and building laws and permits needed to initiate new construction.

Preservationists are often architects who have typically completed a combination of undergraduate and graduate study leading to a degree in architecture. Others have advanced degrees in historic preservation and architectural history. Those entering the field can also benefit from experience with construction administration and computer-aided design (CAD).

Some experts say that preservation and renovation of existing buildings will make up between 30 and 50 percent of all building services in the United States by 2010, and employment for all architects is expected to grow over the next 10 years. This field tends to attract highly motivated professionals interested in history and experienced in architecture and general construction.

find your future

roofer

roofer While other construction specialists are responsible for providing solid ground beneath your feet, roofers are the professionals who keep a roof over your head—whether you're at home, at school, or in a public building. They not only know how to build, maintain, and repair roofs, but they know all the possible materials that can be used to cover a roof, including tile, slate, wood, asphalt, metals, plastics, and more.

The most important quality of these materials is that they protect the inside of a building from the wind, rain, and sun. A poorly constructed roof can lead to water damage that can ruin furniture, walls, flooring, equipment, and belongings and can even compromise the structural integrity of a building.

Building a proper roof is a bit like making a many layered sandwich. For most commercial buildings, the process often begins by placing a layer of insulation, which is then spread over with a layer of hot molten *bitumen*. Bitumen seals over cracks and openings and helps to adhere the next layer of *roofing felt*, a fabric that is soaked in more bitumen. Using a mop, roofers than spread on more hot bitumen to make the roof watertight. The roofer will put down several layers like this (called

Search It!
National Roofing Contractors Association (NRCA) at **www.nrca.net**

Read It!
Professional Roofing at **www.professionalroofing.net** or receive a free brochure on careers in roofing from the NRCA by calling (888) ROOF-321.

Learn It!
- On-the-job training program or three-year apprenticeship program
- Trade, technical, or vocational school courses

Earn It!
Median annual salary is $36,836. (Source: NRCA Salary and Benefits Survey)

Find It!
Look for leads with the Roof Coatings Manufacturers Association (**www.roofcoatings.org**) or the Roof Consultants Institute (**www.rci-online.org**).

Get Started Now!

To go up the ladder in a roofing career, start now by doing the following:

- Take courses in mathematics, blueprint reading, and general shop.
- Those who go on to specialize in metal roofing can benefit from courses about metal craftsmanship and learning construction basics such as welding.
- The summer months are more popular for roofing jobs than the winter and students can often find part-time work as roofing assistants during these months.

Hire Yourself!

Your school has an old garage with a roof measuring 50 feet by 35 feet. The roof has three air vents measuring 2 feet by 2.5 feet and a skylight measuring 3 feet by 3.5 feet. The school has come to you to find out the exact square footage of rubber they will need to cover that area. Prepare an estimate listing your calculations. For extra credit, give a list of local shops that carry roofing supplies and suggest other types of covering besides rubber that the schools might consider.

plies) and then top it off with a glazed or gravel-embedded top layer of hot bitumen. Sometimes, the final top cover is a sheet of waterproof rubber or thermoplastic.

For homes, shingles made from a variety of materials are typically installed as the final top layer. This work can be a bit of a puzzle as roofers cut shingles to fit around chimneys and vent pipes. Depending on where roofers work, they may have to take extra precautions and follow stricter building codes. Roofers in hurricane-prone areas secure roofing much more strongly to withstand catastrophic weather.

More than most construction careers, roofers expose themselves to all types of weather conditions and their jobs can be especially challenging in the hot weather. Not only do they work under the bright sun, they also typically apply hot tar and bitumen. Additional exertion comes from operating hoists and lifts, compressors, and shingle-removing equipment. Those with a fear of heights need not apply for a roofing job for obvious reasons. These craftsmen spend long hours climbing up ladders to work sites at varying heights. They often depend on a keen sense of balance, positioning themselves on scaffolding at 45-degree angles (or more).

Basic math and geometry skills are important to measure roofing materials to cover a certain square footage. Precise measuring and cutting comes into play to make shingles fit perfectly on a roof. Most roofers learn the trade through apprenticeships or trade schools, but education is ongoing and because new roofing products continually come on the market, professionals have to stay informed of current trends.

Roofing is very hard work, so turnover is high. But the good news is that opportunities are usually plentiful and the job is virtually recession-proof.

find your safety director future

safety director

There's an accident on the job site. One of your workers has taken a nasty fall and has broken several bones. The construction company has to help pay his medical bills—and pay someone new to take his place. Meanwhile, the employee suffers through painful medical treatments while wondering if he'll ever be well enough to work again. He also questions how to prevent this type of accident from occurring again—a question that can be answered by a safety director.

A safety director's ultimate goal is to study a work site and create a safety plan that covers virtually every area of that site. They analyze data from similar sites, including accident reports, and help ensure that similar accidents don't happen. They then help train employees in important safety procedures. Directors must follow stringent regulations set by the government's Occupational Safety and Health Administration (OSHA).

The precautions that safety directors check on differ from site to site. For example, safety experts may make sure that builders working on high scaffolding are wearing safety harnesses. Scaffolding must be secure to walk on and free of debris. For workers laying asphalt (pavement) on a roof or road, precautions must be taken to limit exposure to the dangerous material. This includes keeping the asphalt at the right

Search It!
Visit the Construction Safety Council at ***www.buildsafe.org***

Read It!
Read sample articles from the *Professional Safety Journal* at ***www.asse.org/professional_ safety_frameset.html***

Learn It!
- An associate or bachelor's degree in health and safety
- Construction-related experience

Earn It!
Median annual salary is $46,010. (Source: U.S. Bureau of Labor Statistics)

Find It!
Look for opportunities through the Occupational Safety and Health Administration (***www.osha.gov***).

Get Started Now!

The path to becoming a safety director begins by doing the following:

- Start to get a general knowledge of the construction field, including equipment used.
- Make an assessment of your school's auto or wood shop. Ask the teacher to go over safety procedures with you.
- Call a local construction company or manufacturing plant. Ask if you can interview the safety director about what precautions are most important in their work.

Hire Yourself!

You've been hired as a safety director on a building project. A 30-story apartment building is being erected. Laborers will be operating cranes to transport steel to workers on a high scaffold. Ironworkers will be cutting and welding the steel. Additionally, the high building is very close to a city power line. What steps should you take as a safety director to ensure the security of the workers? Create a one-page safety bulletin outlining your suggestions.

temperature and wearing protective gear, such as goggles and masks. For workers in loud construction zones, a safety director might seek out newer, quieter equipment models, provide earplugs, and measure the decibel level of the site. Other safety issues involve protection against fire, toxic substances, and electrocution, and the proper use of equipment, from bulldozers and cranes to hammers and nails.

Safety directors don't just protect employees from injury or death; they protect employers from financial ruin. A construction company found liable in an accident can lose millions of dollars. Random site inspections performed by OSHA can result in high fines if safety guidelines are not followed. For example, a company was penalized almost $200,000 after a worker was burned while working on electrical equipment—because he wasn't properly trained and didn't have the right safety gear.

Safety directors usually learn their particular skills on the job, often beginning as part of a safety staff. They may also start their careers as construction laborers and decide to pursue work concerning the safety side of a job site. Training may involve taking OSHA-sponsored workshops, and a college degree in occupational health can be especially helpful for gaining employment. Similar careers include building and fire inspectors.

Construction workers often toil in dangerous work environments under strenuous conditions, but it's the safety director's job to help keep those workers out of harm's way—setting up precautionary measures that can save lives every year.

find your scheduler future

Search It!
The International Professional Construction Estimators Association at ***www.pcea.org***

Read It!
Select articles from *Engineering News Record* can be read at ***www.enr.com/news***

Learn It!
- College degree in an engineering discipline is recommended
- Construction work experience

Earn It!
Median annual salary is $53,984. (Source: Salary.com)

Find It!
Look into job opportunities at major firms like McGraw-Hill Construction (***www.construction.com***) or check listings at ***www. constructionweblinks.com***.

scheduler

You get to school at 8:00 in the morning, go to math from 8:15 to 9:30, history from 9:38 to 10:53, Spanish from 11:01 to 12:16, then lunch, P.E., chemistry, until eventually that bell rings to signify your freedom. Your school day is organized into very distinct blocks of time to ensure that everything has a time and a place. And, quite often, one class must be taken before another: pre-algebra before algebra, for instance. Who comes up with this schedule? Probably you and your guidance counselor. A construction scheduling engineer does something similar—he or she compiles a list of tasks for a given project, and assigns a duration of time to each, so that the project can be completed on time.

A scheduling engineer, or project scheduler, has the job of planning and scheduling the activities of a construction project's work crew. The scheduler wants to devise the most efficient schedule possible, since longer (or slower) projects equal greater costs.

Get Started Now!

Try these strategies to prepare for a career in construction scheduling:

- A good scheduler must be computer-savvy. Take computer classes offered at your school, and play around with different programs at home.
- Start making the most of your time by using a calendar or student planner to keep track of assignments, activities, and appointments. For information about a highly respected personal organization system, go on-line to the Franklin Covey website at ***www.franklincovey.com***.
- Contact a local contracting firm, and see if you can speak to a scheduler or shadow him or her at work for a day.
- Volunteer to help your guidance counselor prepare student schedules for next semester.

Hire Yourself!

Your school is having a fund-raiser, and, at the last minute, you have been asked to bring in two cakes for the cake walk. They must be made quickly and be finished at the same time since you're under a time crunch. Pick two different cakes. Go on-line and find recipes (try *www.foodtv.com*), then devise a schedule for each one, assuming you have all the ingredients you'd need. Pick a time to start, and figure out what tasks you'd be performing (pre-heating the oven, greasing the pan, sifting the flour, etc.), the sequence of those tasks, the duration, and the lag time between each. Time it so both come out of the oven at roughly the same time. Record the resulting task schedule in an easy to read chart.

Most schedulers today create a schedule using the Critical Path Method (CPM). A CPM schedule is essentially a way of determining the least amount of time needed for a project's completion, based on the order of tasks (the "path"), and the amount of time needed to complete each one. There are software programs that do the painful work for schedulers; Primavera SureTrak and Microsoft Project are names of just two.

But before a scheduler uses any sort of computer program, he or she should make a preliminary schedule in the bid phase of a project. (You can't submit a bid for a project without a schedule that tells you how long it will take, and thus how much—roughly—the project will cost.) The first step in this process is to list the activities to be completed. For example, for a house-building project, a few of the many activities might include framing, roofing, HVAC (heating, ventilation, and air-conditioning) facilities, drywall installation, ceiling finish, and painting. Many of these activities must be done in a certain order. For instance, you cannot install ceiling without first installing a framework. A scheduler lists these tasks and puts them in order.

Once they are in order, the scheduler inputs this information into a computer. He or she assigns one of the following connections to each activity: finish to start; finish to finish; or start to start. Finish to start means that the completion of the previous task will determine when the next will start. finish to finish means the current task's completion will depend on the preceding one's completion. Start to start—you may have guessed—means that the beginning of one task depends on that of the one that precedes it on the list. Then, lag, or the amount of time between each activity, and duration are determined. If the project needs to be accelerated, the scheduler will decide then how this should be done: overtime, extra shifts, etc. And here's some good news: For each new project, if the scheduler has worked on one similar to it, he or she can use their previous work as a template!

Schedulers may work on one or several projects at a time, depending on how much they like to have on their plate at one time, how complex a given project is, and how they are employed. Some work as independent consultants, and others as salaried employees at construction firms.

It used to be the case that schedulers needed only to have several years' experience working in some capacity of the construction industry. It's becoming more common, however, for schedulers to have a degree in engineering, architecture, or construction management. A scheduler must be familiar with construction terminology, practice, and culture, as well as be able to decipher construction sketches. Schedulers also have the opportunity to advance in the industry—it's not uncommon for them to go on to become superintendents, project managers, and project executives.

Are you well-organized? Do you have a knack for figuring out the best way to get something done? If so, then you may want to schedule some time to look into a career in construction scheduling.

Search It!
The National Society of
Professional Surveyors at
www.acsm.net/nsps

Read It!
*Professional Surveyor Magazine
Online* at *www.profsurv.com*

Learn It!
- An associate's or bachelor's
  degree in surveying or a similar
  concentration, and extensive on-
  the-job training is becoming the
  norm
- Find schools offering degrees in
  surveying at *www.acsm.net/
  abetlisting.html*

Earn It!
Median annual salary is $39,970.
(Source: U.S. Bureau of Labor
Statistics)

Find It!
To get an idea of available jobs,
visit *www.lsrp.com/posavil.
html*.

find your surveyor future

surveyor

In 1966, NASA launched the first U.S. spacecraft to ever land safely on the moon. Its job: to determine if the surface of the moon was safe for human landing. Its name: *Surveyor*. Just as *Surveyor* measured the moon's surface, professional surveyors on this planet measure and map the earth's surface. They also find and set boundaries, and prepare detailed reports on land to be used for the construction of buildings, airports, and more. Their descriptions of land may go into deeds, leases, and other legal documents.

A surveyor's job is not exactly a walk in the park, even though it may sometimes *require* a walk in the park. Before visiting a site, these professionals must first research the location to see if there are any existing boundaries. The surveyor is then responsible for leading a party of technicians and assistants into the field where they analyze every aspect of the land being studied—its shape, its cracks, slopes, and slants. They take notes, make sketches, and enter data into computers.

To get precise measurements, they depend on instruments such as the theodolite (used for gauging horizontal and vertical angles), sophisticated electronic distance-measuring equipment, and even geographic information systems (GIS), computerized data banks of "spatial data."

Get Started Now!

Start preparing for a career as a surveyor:
- Take classes such as algebra, trigonometry, drafting, mechanical drawing, and computer science.
- Hiking and camping can help give you experience walking miles and carrying heavy equipment. Make note of distances walked and the general topography, whether it's flat, hilly, or rugged terrain.
- Participate in a school club or activity that allows you to work hands-on with a group, like a science club or intramural sport.

Hire Yourself!

A local surveyor wants to hire you to help him survey a plot of land. As a test, he has asked you to choose a plot of land and make a detailed report. Choose a defined area, such as the school parking lot or a playground, and write as many details as possible describing it—any areas where the land slopes, large rock formations or cracks, the size of the land, etc. Include a photo or a drawing showing these characteristics. (Perhaps use graph paper to chart it out.) Visit *www.lsrp.com/lot.pdf* for an example of a land survey.

Sometimes, surveyors use photographic equipment, and even take aerial photographs from airplanes, to ensure accurate records. For larger projects, surveyors may turn to the latest in global positioning systems (GPS). The same type of satellite technology used in many new cars to get instant directions can also be used to help measure the earth's surface.

Sixty percent of surveyors work for architectural firms, but others specialize in areas such as *marine surveying* (exploring bodies of water) and *geophysical prospecting* (typically studying land that will be drilled for petroleum). Some go on to related careers in cartography and photogrammetry. Like surveyors, cartographers study land, but use the data to produce maps. Similarly, *photogrammetrists* create maps from aerial photographs.

In addition to earning a degree in surveying or a related subject, these professionals must get extensive on-the-job training and pass a state licensing exam. Not only do they need keen mathematical ability and map-making knowledge, they must also be in good physical shape to lug heavy equipment in the outdoors and often over rugged terrain. Accuracy, above all else, is perhaps the most important trait of the surveyor. Without correct measurements, a home could be placed on land where it doesn't belong or on land that is unstable. That's why surveyors are such important members of a construction team.

If you have an eye for detail, a brain for geography, and a keen attention to details, a career in surveying may be for you. Those who become surveyors join the illustrious ranks of some of the country's most famous surveyors: George Washington, Abraham Lincoln, Henry Thoreau, and Daniel Boone.

Search It!

The American Planning Association at **www.planning.org**

Read It!

The Association of Collegiate Schools of Planning *Update* at **www.acsp.org/news/news.htm** and *Practicing Planner* at **www. planning.org/practicingplanner/ default1.htm**

Learn It!

- A master's degree in city planning or urban design
- Some entry-level jobs demand only a bachelor's degree

Earn It!

Median annual salary is $49,880. (Source: U.S. Bureau of Labor Statistics)

Find It!

For information on job availability, as well as certification, scholarships, and a list of schools offering planning degrees, visit **www. acsp.org**.

urban planner

The residents of Anytown, U.S.A., are concerned about its future. They worry that if many new homes are erected, too many people will live there. Schools will become overcrowded. There won't be enough open spaces, like parks and playgrounds. The roads will become congested with traffic. To help prevent these problems, the mayor decides to hire an urban planner.

Urban planners analyze an area's problems and needs to create the best use of available space. While often referred to as *urban planners*, these professionals can work for local governments in suburban towns and rural areas as well as in cities.

The first thing a planner does is complete a report on the current use of the land. They study the placement and capacity of streets, highways, and water and sewer lines. They also report on the number of structures like homes, businesses, schools, and houses of worship. Additionally, a planner needs to know about the people who live in the city. For example, what types of jobs do they have? How many families with school-age children are there?

After completing their research and speaking with resident groups, public officials, civic leaders, and land developers, the planner can get to work on a proposal for uses of the land.

Get Started Now!

- Take classes in economics, social studies, and statistics. These will help you analyze the characteristics of a community.
- Work on your writing and public speaking skills. Planners need to be able to communicate well.
- Computer skills are also a must, especially GIS, a computer system for studying geographical information.

114

Hire Yourself!

A large discount store chain wants to open a new store in a town where you are the planner. Opponents say the store will increase traffic and threaten local businesses. Supporters say it will create jobs and be a convenient place to shop. The town council has hired you to help them decide whether the store should be built. Make your decision and write down a list of 10 new reasons (other than those already mentioned) to support it or oppose it.

As large cities, like New York and San Francisco, become more expensive to live in, more people who work in those cities move to surrounding towns. A planner may help design train lines or bus systems to help residents of far-away towns get to work more easily.

One of the greatest success stories in urban planning was the creation of Central Park in 1853. The 843-acre space provides a much needed natural refuge where city dwellers can find recreation and escape from the urban landscape. More recently, planners for cities such as Charleston, South Carolina, and San Antonio, Texas, have planned revitalized waterfront areas, complete with shopping, boat rides, theaters, and restaurants to attract tourists and residents alike.

To really advance in this field, you'll need a master's degree in urban planning or a similar field, such as geography, urban design, or civil engineering. Computer proficiency is a must for analyzing data and creating 3-D models, for example. Seventy percent of planners work for local governments, although jobs as consultants working for private industry are expected to increase.

So what happened to Anytown, U.S.A.? With a planner's help, the town government decided to use available funds to build an extension on the school. They also reduced the number of building permits awarded to construction companies and designated an area of land that must be preserved as a green space.

No community can solve all of its problems, but with the help of a planner, any city or town can become a better place to live.

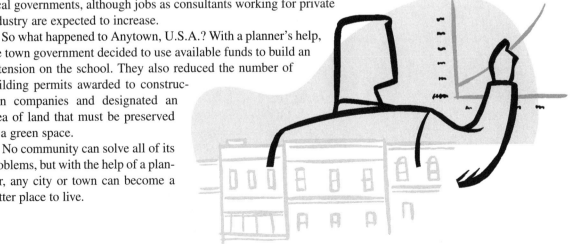

Search It!
American Water Works
Association at ***www.awwa.org***
and Water Environment Federation
at ***www.wef.org***

Read It!
Opflow Online at ***www.awwa.
org/communications/opflow***
and *Water Week* at ***www.awwa.
org/communications/
waterweek***

Learn It!
● High school diploma
● On-the-job training
● Associate's degree provides a
  competitive edge

Earn It!
Median annual salary is $33,390.
(Source: U.S. Bureau of Labor
Statistics)

Find It!
To find information about current
employment opportunities, visit the
job board at the Water
Environment Federation (***www.
wef.org/careeropps***).

find your future
wastewater maintenance technician

wastewater maintenance technician

Americans use 339 billion gallons of water *every day* for common tasks like taking showers, cooking food, and going to the bathroom. What happens to all that dirty water? Before that water is directed back into our rivers, oceans, and streams, it must pass through treatment plants where wastewater experts remove dangerous pollutants. Wastewater contains harmful bacteria that can cause disease and kill fish if it were to reach the main water supply.

Anytime you take a shower, wash the dishes, or flush the toilet, the wastewater you create flows through the pipes in your home, to the pipes of your town's sewer system. (Some small towns don't have sewer systems, in which case each home takes care of their own wastewater through the use of a septic tank.) The pipes transport the wastewater to a wastewater treatment facility. This is where wastewater maintenance technicians do their job.

Get Started Now!
● Classes in biology, chemistry, and mathematics will help you prepare for a job in wastewater operations.
● Join an organization dedicated to helping the environment. This will help you learn about the problems facing our water supply.
● Water treatment plants increasingly rely on computer technology to manage their operations. Becoming familiar with computer basics can be helpful.

Hire Yourself!

You're a wastewater maintenance technicians at a local treatment plant. Your boss asks you to design a training diagram for new employees showing the process that wastewater goes through, beginning in a home and ending, clean, in a river or ocean. Using research from the Internet and books from the library, draw a basic diagram.

These technicians are responsible for working the pumps, valves, and other equipment that move the water through various stages of treatment. They must read and adjust meters and gauges to make sure equipment is operating correctly. The cleansing process takes place in several tanks—one tank separates solids from liquids. Another tank is where solids are broken down, heating some of it into gas that is used as an energy source by the treatment facility. In yet another tank, chlorine and other chemicals are added to the water to remove bacteria and viruses. Technicians may also perform maintenance on the equipment and test water for contaminants. Their tests will assure that water is being properly cleaned to meet federal environmental guidelines.

Controlling sophisticated treatment equipment requires a strong background in math and computers. Since the cleaning process involves chemicals, professionals rely on knowledge of chemistry and biology as well. Treatment facilities have improved over the years, but there are still areas that will be noisy, dirty, and smelly—they do, after all, deal with human waste.

Technicians start out as trainees and must take a certification exam. Advanced certifications are also available that allow operators to work on more advanced equipment. Eventually, they may become a superintendent or supervisor.

A similar job to wastewater maintenance technician is that of water treatment operators. These workers make water from rivers, streams, wells, and reservoirs safe for drinking by removing contaminants like microorganisms and lead. Some wastewater maintenance technicians are also water treatment operators, and their roles often overlap.

Job availability is expected to remain good in the future. Most technicians work for local governments, but jobs in private industry are on the rise. Wastewater maintenance technicians may not have glamorous jobs, but their work makes the world's water safer for wildlife and humans alike.

Big Question #5:
do you have the right skills?

Career exploration is, in one sense, career matchmaking. The goal is to match your basic traits, interests and strengths, work values, and work personality with viable career options.

But the "stuff" you bring to a job is only half of the story.

Choosing an ideal job and landing your dream job is a two-way street. Potential employers look for candidates with specific types of skills and backgrounds. This is especially true in our technology-infused, global economy.

In order to find the perfect fit, you need to be fully aware of not only what you've got, but also what prospective employers need.

The following activity is designed to help you accomplish just that. This time we'll use the "wannabe" approach —working with careers you think you want to consider. This same matchmaking process will come in handy when it comes time for the real thing too.

Unfortunately, this isn't one of those "please turn to the end of the chapter and you'll find all the answers" types of activities. This one requires the best critical thinking, problem-solving, and decision-making skills you can muster.

Big Activity #5:
do you have the right skills?

Here's how it works:

Step 1: First, make a chart like the one on page 120.

Step 2: Next, pick a career profile that interests you and use the following resources to compile a list of the traits and skills needed to be successful. Include:

- Information featured in the career profile in this book;
- Information you discover when you look through websites of any of the professional associations or other resources listed with each career profile;
- Information from the career profiles and skills lists found on-line at America's Career InfoNet at *www.acinet.org*.

Briefly list the traits or skills you find on separate lines in the first column of your chart.

Step 3: Evaluate yourself as honestly as possible. If, after careful consideration, you conclude that you already possess one of the traits or skills included on your list, place an *X* in the column marked "Got It!" If you conclude that the skill or trait is one you've yet to acquire, follow these directions to complete the column marked "Get It?":

- If you believe that gaining proficiency in a skill is just a matter of time and experience and you're willing to do whatever it takes to acquire that skill, place a *Y* (for yes) in the corresponding space.
- Or, if you are quite certain that a particular skill is one that you don't possess now, and either can't or won't do what it takes to acquire it, mark the corresponding space with an *N* (for no). For example, you want to be a brain surgeon. It's important, prestigious work and the pay is good. But, truth be told, you'd rather have brain surgery yourself than sit through eight more years of really intense science and math. This rather significant factor may or may not affect your ultimate career choice. But it's better to think it through now rather than six years into med school.

Step 4: Place your completed chart in your Big Question AnswerBook.

When you work through this process carefully, you should get some eye-opening insights into the kinds of careers that are right for you. Half reality check and half wake-up call, this activity lets you see how you measure up against important workforce competencies.

Big Activity #5: **do you have the right skills?**

skill or trait required	got it!	get it!

more
career ideas in
architecture and
construction

Careers featured in the previous section represent mainstream, highly viable occupations where someone with the right set of skills and training stands more than half a chance of finding gainful employment. However, these ideas are just the beginning. There are lots of ways to make a living in any industry—and this one is no exception.

Following is a list of career ideas related in one way or another to the construction and architecture industries. This list is included here for two reasons. First, to illustrate some unique ways to blend your interests with opportunities. Second, to keep you thinking beyond the obvious.

As you peruse the list you're sure to encounter some occupations you've never heard of before. We hope you get curious enough to look them up. Others may trigger one of those "aha" moments where everything clicks and you know you're onto something good. Either way we hope it helps point the way toward some rewarding opportunities in construction and architecture.

Bricklayer	Electronic Systems Technician
Cabinetmaker	Equipment Operator
Construction Engineer	Expeditor
Construction Project Engineer	Fabricator
Constructor	Field Engineer
Drywall Finisher	Field Technician
Drywall Installer	Fire Prevention and Protection Engineer
Education and Training Director	
Electrical Sub Assembler	Furniture Maker

General Maintenance Mechanic

General Manager

Glass Cutter

Glass Rigger

Heavy Equipment Mechanic

Highway Construction Worker

Highway Design Manager

Hydro Testing Technician

Industrial Engineer

Information Systems Manager

Inspector

Insulation Worker

Line Assemblyman

Machinist

Maintenance Planner

Manufacturer's Representative

Mapping Technician

Marble Setter

Marketing Manager

Materials Engineer

Mechanical Drafter

Metalworker

Millwright

Modeler

Operations Engineer

Paperhanger

Parts Manager

Parts Warehouse Clerk

Pipefitter

Power Saw Operator

Press Brake Operator

Project Manager

Property Manager

Purchasing Agent

Real Estate Agent

Receiving Clerk

Refractory Technician

Regional Planner

Renderer

Road Crew Worker

Sales Manager

Sales Representative

Sander

Security Specialist

Service Manager

Shear Operator

Sheet Metal Worker

Shipping Clerk

Speciality Contractor

Steamfitter

Stockroom Attendant

Straightening Press Operator

Structural Engineer

Superintendent

Thermal Control Technician

Tile Setter

Traffic Engineer

Transportation Manager

Utility Operator

Utility Repairperson

Welder

Big Question #6:
are you on the right path?

You've covered a lot of ground so far. You've had a chance to discover more about your own potential and expectations. You've taken some time to explore the realities of a wide variety of career opportunities within this industry.

Now is a good time to sort through all the details and figure out what all this means to you. This process involves equal measures of input from your head and your heart. Be honest, think big, and, most of all, stay true to you.

You may be considering an occupation that requires years of advanced schooling which, from your point of view, seems an insurmountable hurdle. What do you do? Give up before you even get started? We hope not. We'd suggest that you try some creative thinking.

Big Activity #6:
are you on the right path?

Start by asking yourself if you want to pursue this particular career so badly that you're willing to do whatever it takes to make it. Then stretch your thinking a little to consider alternative routes, nontraditional career paths, and other equally meaningful occupations.

Following are some prompts to help you sort through your ideas. Simply jot down each prompt on a separate sheet of notebook paper and leave plenty of space for your responses.

Big Activity #6: **are you on the right path?**

One thing I know for sure about my future occupation is

I'd prefer to pursue a career that offers

I'd prefer to pursue a career that requires

A career option I'm now considering is

What appeals to me most about this career is

What concerns me most about this career is

Things that I still need to learn about this career include

Big Activity #6: **are you on the right path?**

Another career option I'm considering is

What appeals to me most about this career is

What concerns me most about this career is

Things that I still need to learn about this career include

Of these two career options I've named, the one that best fits most of my interests, skills, values, and work personality is   because

At this point in the process, I am

❏ Pretty sure I'm on the right track

❏ Not quite sure yet but still interested in exploring some more

❏ Completely clueless about what I want to do

SECTION 3

experiment with success

Right about now you may find it encouraging to learn that the average person changes careers five to seven times in his or her life. Plus, most college students change majors several times. Even people who are totally set on what they want to do often end up being happier doing something just a little bit different from what they first imagined.

So, whether you think you've found the ultimate answer to career happiness or you're just as confused as ever, you're in good company. The best advice for navigating these important life choices is this: Always keep the door open to new ideas.

As smart and dedicated as you may be, you just can't predict the future. Some of the most successful professionals in any imaginable field could never ever have predicted what—and how—they would be doing what they actually do today. Why? Because when they were in high school those jobs didn't even exist. It was not too long ago that there were no such things as personal computers, Internet research, digital cameras, mass e-mails, cell phones, or any of the other newfangled tools that are so critical to so many jobs today.

Keeping the door open means being open to recognizing changes in yourself as you mature and being open to changes in the way the world works. It also involves a certain willingness to learn new things and tackle new challenges.

It's easy to see how being open to change can sometimes allow you to go further in your chosen career than you ever dreamed. For instance, in almost any profession you can imagine, technology has fueled unprecedented opportunities. Those people and companies who have embraced this "new way of working" have often surpassed their original expectations of success. Just ask Bill Gates. He's now one of the world's wealthiest men thanks to a company called Microsoft that he cofounded while still a student at Harvard University.

It's a little harder to see, but being open to change can also mean that you may have to let go of your first dream and find a more appropriate one. Maybe your dream is to become a professional athlete. At this point in your life you may think that there's nothing in the world that would possibly make you happier. Maybe you're right and maybe you have the talent and persistence (and the lucky breaks) to take you all the way.

But maybe you don't. Perhaps if you opened yourself to new ideas you'd discover that the best career involves blending your interest in sports with your talent in writing to become a sports journalist or sports information director. Maybe your love of a particular sport and your interest in working with children might best be served in a coaching career. Who knows what you might achieve when you open yourself to all the possibilities?

So, whether you've settled on a career direction or you are still not sure where you want to go, there are several "next steps" to consider. In this section, you'll find three more Big Questions to help keep your career planning moving forward. These Big Questions are:

❷ Big Question #7: **who knows what you need to know?**

❷ Big Question #8: **how can you find out what a career is really like?**

❷ Big Question #9: **how do you know when you've made the right choice?**

Big Question #7:
who knows what
you need to know?

When it comes to the nitty-gritty details about what a particular job is really like, who knows what you need to know? Someone with a job like the one you want, of course. They'll have the inside scoop—important information you may never find in books or websites. So make talking to as many people as you can part of your career planning process.

Learn from them how they turned their own challenges into opportunities, how they got started, and how they made it to where they are now. Ask the questions that aren't covered in "official" resources, such as what's it really like to do their job, how they manage to do a good job and have a great life, how they learned what they needed to learn to do their job well, and the best companies or situations to start in.

A good place to start with these career chats or "informational interviews" is with people you know—or more likely, people you know who know people with jobs you find interesting. People you already know include your parents (of course), relatives, neighbors, friends' parents, people who belong to your place of worship or club, and so on.

All it takes to get the process going is gathering up all your nerve and asking these people for help. You'll find that nine and a half times out of 10, the people you encounter will be delighted to help, either by providing information about their careers or by introducing you to people they know who can help.

experiment with success

hints and tips for a successful interview

● TIP #1
Think about your goals for the interview, and write them down.

Be clear about what you want to know after the interview that you didn't know before it.

Remember that the questions for all personal interviews are not the same. You would probably use different questions to write a biography of the person, to evaluate him or her for a job, to do a history of the industry, or to learn about careers that might interest you.

Writing down your objectives will help you stay focused.

● TIP #2
Pay attention to how you phrase your questions.

Some questions that we ask people are "closed" questions; we are looking for a clear answer, not an elaboration. "What time does the movie start?" is a good example of a closed question.

Sometimes, when we ask a closed question, we shortchange ourselves. Think about the difference between "What times are the showings tonight?" and "Is there a 9 P.M. showing?" By asking the second question, you may not find out if there is an 8:45 or 9:30 show.

That can be frustrating. It usually seems so obvious when we ask a question that we expect a full answer. It's important to remember, though, that the person hearing the question doesn't always have the same priorities or know why the question is being asked.

The best example of this? Think of the toddler who answers the phone. When the caller asks, "Is your mom home?" the toddler says, "Yes" and promptly hangs up. Did the child answer the question? As far as he's concerned, he did a great job!

Another problem with closed questions is that they sometimes require so many follow-up questions that the person being interviewed feels like a suspect in an interrogation room.

A series of closed questions may go this way:

Q: What is your job title?
A: Assistant Producer
Q: How long have you had that title?
A: About two years.

Q: What was your title before that?
Q: How long did you have that title?
Q: What is the difference between the two jobs?
Q: What did you do before that?
Q: Where did you learn to do this job?
Q: How did you advance from one job to the next?

An alternative, "open" question invites conversation. An open-question interview might begin this way:

I understand you are an Assistant Producer. I'm really interested in what that job is all about and how you got to be at the level you are today.

Open questions often begin with words like:

Tell me about . . .
How do you feel about . . .
What was it like . . .

● TIP #3

Make the person feel comfortable answering truthfully.
In general, people don't want to say things that they think will make them look bad. How to get at the truth? Be empathic, and make their answers seem "normal."

Ask a performer or artist how he or she feels about getting a bad review from the critics, and you are unlikely to hear, "It really hurts. Sometimes I just want to cry and get out of the business." Or "Critics are so stupid. They never understand what I am trying to do."

Try this approach instead: "So many people in your industry find it hard to deal with the hurt of a bad critical review. How do you handle it when that happens?"

ask the experts

You can learn a lot by interviewing people who are already successful in the types of careers you're interested in. In fact, we followed our own advice and interviewed several people who have been successful in the fields of architecture and construction.

Before you get started on your own interview, take a few minutes to look through the results of some of ours. To make it easier for you to compare the responses of all the people we interviewed, we have presented our interviews as a panel discussion that reveals important success lessons these people have learned along the way. Each panelist is introduced on the next page.

Our interviewees gave us great information about things like what their jobs are really like, how they got to where they are, and even provided a bit of sage advice for people like you who are just getting started.

So Glad You Asked

In addition to the questions we asked in the interviews in this book, you might want to add some of these questions to your own interviews:

- How did your childhood interests relate to your choice of career path?
- How did you first learn about the job you have today?
- In what ways is your job different from how you expected it to be?
- Tell me about the parts of your job that you really like.
- If you could get someone to take over part of your job for you, what aspect would you most like to give up?
- If anything were possible, how would you change your job description?
- What kinds of people do you usually meet in your work?
- Walk me through the whole process of getting your type of product made and distributed. Tell me about all the people who are involved.
- Tell me about the changes you have seen in your industry over the years. What do you see as the future of the industry?
- Are there things you would do differently in your career if you could do it all over?

real people with real jobs in architecture and construction

Following are introductions to our panel of experts. Get acquainted with their backgrounds and then use their job titles to track their stories throughout the five success lessons.

Robert Decker

Christine Hess

Stacey Hovis

Isaac Panzarella

JP Reuer

- **Candace Cain** lives in Seminole, Oklahoma, where she is owner and **Construction Manager** of two companies, Garcia Construction and Dirtwork and Design.
- **Robert Decker** is a corporate **Equipment Manager** in Pittsburgh, Pennsylvania.
- **Susan Flashman** works as a union journeyman **Electrician** in Mount Rainer, Maryland.
- **Patricia Galloway** is the chief executive officer (**CEO**) of the Nielson-Wurster Group, an engineering and management consulting company in Seattle, Washington.
- **Christine Hess** is **Career Education Director** for Associated Builders and Contractors, a national trade association based in Arlington, Virginia.
- **Stacey Hovis** is a **Marketing Manager** for Kajima Construction Service in Atlanta, Georgia.
- **Isaac Panzarella** is a "green" **Mechanical Engineer** of buildings and building systems. He lives and works in Raleigh, North Carolina.
- **JP Reuer** is an **Architect** working in Doha, Qatar as a visiting professor with the Virginia Commonwealth University.

Everybody has to start somewhere!

Following is a list of first jobs once held by our esteemed panel of experts.

Mechanic

Head usher

Stage manager

Box office assistant

Tunnel inspector

Teacher

Baby-sitter

Retail salesclerk

Carpenter's helper

Dishwasher

Parks and recreation counselor

Success Lesson #1:

Work is a good thing when you find the right career.

- ## Tell us what it's like to work in your current career.

Construction Manager: My companies perform civil work. To put it bluntly, we are the dirt crew. We build the roadbed up to grade. Some day I hope to actually be building the bridges but for now I am content to be on the jobsite and watching. I actually work on my jobsites. I do every job that is required of me, from foreperson to dump truck driver to equipment operator. I am learning quickly.

Equipment Manager: I manage a fleet of heavy equipment along with a fleet of support vehicles. My job also involves purchasing, selling, and trading equipment. I have a support staff of six and I manage 25 mechanics.

Electrician: While union journeyman electricians may work on residential, commercial, and industrial electrical installations, I work primarily on new commercial installations. It is very physical work, involving climbing ladders, stairs, and scaffolds, and carrying materials and equipment. The work may require dealing with the weather, in exposed or semi-exposed locations for eight hours a day. The work can also be very challenging mentally, because it will often involve trouble-shooting—finding the source of a problem and correcting it.

CEO: I perform risk management and dispute resolution. Risk management is done at the front end and during a construction project. The process assists the client in determining what risks exist that could cause a project to either cost more or be delayed and it puts in place monitoring measures to either reduce or minimize the risk. In the dispute resolution area, I serve as an expert witness and evaluate projects to determine what went wrong and why and who is responsible. My area of specialty is project controls with a concentration on delay—or why projects take longer to complete than planned.

Marketing Manager: I am responsible for tracking leads to new projects for our construction firm either through reports or through word of mouth from networking contacts. I then must determine if the potential project is a good fit for our firm. Since we mostly do industrial work, I wouldn't look at a lead for a hotel as a good fit. Once we determine if the lead is "hot," we then submit an RFQ (Request for Qualifications). This is like a report or "sales pitch" about our firm. Of course, there could be as many as 20 firms chasing the same project, so only the most qualified firms are invited to submit an RFP (Request for Proposal). Once the owner reviews the price and the qualifications, a general contractor will be selected or awarded the project.

However, at this point I am already trying to qualify new leads. My main responsibility is building the "right" relationships with other people in the industry. These relationships are key because they can alert you to an upcoming project before it hits the street. I must attend meetings with different trade associations, and visit as many architects and owners as possible.

Mechanical Engineer: I am a freelance designer, meaning I have my own company. This doesn't mean I work alone; I work on various projects with other designers with other areas of expertise, such as architects or civil engineers.

My responsibility on a project team includes design of the systems in a building, which includes heating and cooling, plumbing and electrical power, and lighting. There is an important aspect to my approach to this work in that I try to design buildings that are environmentally friendly and healthy for people to inhabit.

Architect: I design buildings—mostly houses and small apartment complexes. Occasionally, I also manage the construction of the building.

Success Lesson #2:
Career goals change and so do you.

- ### When you were in high school, what career did you hope to pursue?

Construction Manager: I made the choice at a very young age to stand up and take responsibility for my own life. I looked around me and watched as other kids my age were partying and playing. They were able to do that, most of the time because their parents supported them. I didn't want my parents' help or money. I wanted something that was mine and I have been making it happen ever since.

Equipment Manager: Growing up, I was always interested in how things worked, such as toy cars and trucks. I began my career as a mechanic.

Electrician: In high school, I wanted to be a theatrical set designer, stage manager, or technical staff person.

CEO: I had no idea I would be an engineer when I was a teenager. I thought I would be an interpreter for the United Nations or an interior designer.

Career Education Director: I wanted to be a graphic designer or industrial designer. I have always been very artistic. However, I went to school at night and worked full time during the day. A business class was two hours long and an art class took hours each session. With my limited time available, I took a short cut and went in the direction of marketing and public relations. I figured you had to have a creative mind to work in this arena too, and I was right.

Mechanical Engineer: During my last two years of high school, I had the wonderful opportunity to work as an engineering co-op student for General Motors. This program was designed to give young people an idea of what it really is like to have a career in the real world. We had the chance to sign up for assignments in several different departments, so I learned about different types of work and in the end decided that I would like to be a mechanical engineer.

Architect: I think I always envisioned doing something somewhat creative and something in which I could make a difference. It has taken a long time to get comfortable with my career and I have tried many other things along the way. I think the "detours" have been helpful.

- ## What was it that made you change directions?

Equipment Manager: After working at various companies, several of my employers saw the manager material I had within me. With more schooling in labor management I worked my way up to the area that I am in today.

Electrician: The change from theater came out of the knowledge that I needed more from my four year degree in political science and sociology. But my "dream" of perhaps going to law school or even medical school was stunted by the economic realities of my personal situation. However, I am still in a technical field, where I use my hands, as well as my mind.

CEO: When a professor came to our high school when I was a junior, they talked on civil engineering and specifically structural design. Since I used to draw as a hobby I was very interested and decided I would be an engineer.

Career Education Director: Although I couldn't define it exactly at the time, I was looking for a job that would allow me to be creative, to work with people, and to do something different every day.

Marketing Manager: Even though my job is not exactly what I expected to do when I was in high school, marketing still allows me to be very creative since I am often required to put together artistic presentations and programs.

Architect: I wouldn't be doing what I'm doing, or doing it the way I'm doing it, without the mentors and professors that have shared knowledge and time with me. Ultimately, though, I think it's the risks I've taken that I have benefited from the most. These include relocating to unfamiliar places, investing time and energy in projects and design solutions that I believed in, and trusting myself to be able to handle the challenges of unfamiliar situations

Success Lesson #3:
One thing leads to another along any career path.

- **How did you end up doing what you're doing now?**

    CEO: After I started college I realized that I did not especially enjoy structural design. Based on a recommendation from my advisor, I got a double major with my second major in construction. Two events led to the work I'm doing now. One was an early job as a tunnel inspector. The other was working on a major project that involved a lawsuit between the city of Milwaukee and the city of Chicago. These experiences helped me merge my love of engineering and the law.

    Equipment Manager: My work has involved a fairly steady progression up the career ladder. I started by attending tech school during high school. When I was 18 I started working at a car dealership as a "lube" person. After six months I was promoted to line mechanic. Two years later the service manager at the dealership got very sick and told the owner I was the perfect person to replace him as the parts and service manager. Twelve years later I was hired by the owner of a coal surface mine to become their purchasing agent, which led to positions as equipment manager for the coal operation and a promotion to operation manager at their stone quarries. Thirteen years later the Trumbull Corporation offered me a job as their equipment superintendent and later promoted me to the corporate equipment manager position I hold today.

    Career Education Director: Jobs in architecture get scarce when the economy is tight. When I graduated from college with a bachelor of science degree in architecture, jobs were hard to come by. I realized I had to either relocate or take a career "tangent." Boy, am I glad I did! I have the best of all worlds working for a construction association.

    Mechanical Engineer: The occupation I have now is the product of many years of constantly reassessing my situation and taking action to move in a direction that I felt was right. I would ask questions to guide my thinking, such as: What do I like about what I am doing? What are my greatest strengths? How can I make a difference in the world?

Success Lesson #4:
There's more than one way to get an education.

- ● **Where did you learn the skills of your field, both formally (school) and informally (experience)?**

   Construction Manager: I have recently attained an associate's degree in construction management from Oklahoma State University–Okmulgee. This is the second of my two degrees. The first was a general associate of arts degree from Seminole State College. I fully intend to attend Oklahoma State University in the fall to pursue a master's degree in either business administration or heavy highway.

   Equipment Manager: When I worked for the coal company we had a coal workers strike that lasted for three years. As management I had to perform the duties of several workers—operator, manager, worker, truck driver—during the strike. I also had to participate in labor board meetings and attend court hearings. This situation improved my skill set as a manager and I learned a lot about people and working with employees.

   Electrician: Taking drafting in high school helped a lot. Also, building sets for the theater gave me practical experience working with hand tools. In addition, being older than most of my classmates when I went through the apprenticeship gave me greater patience dealing with different types of people who were not all nice.

   CEO: Being involved in professional organizations and their activities is where I learned a lot about leadership, teamwork, and communications.

   Career Education Director: Two things in particular come to mind. The life experience of working with lots of different kinds of people in industries from retail to teaching to office jobs. Also, traveling and seeing things from different perspectives.

   Marketing Manager: I would say that my formal education was very important. However, the learning never really stops: it must be ongoing. Then to succeed in certain roles, you must possess traits that fit with the position. For instance, as a marketing and business development person, it is important that I am outgoing, and comfortable and confident meeting with people.

   Mechanical Engineer: The most important learning experience for me was starting a company immediately after starting college. I had two partners, whom I learned a lot from through their experience. The experience of owning and running a company taught me the value of hard work and how rewarding it can be to be a part of something you own and can be proud of.

Architect: I think I've learned a lot from mistakes I've made. Realizing that it's really up to me to correct them has helped me become more responsible. It has also helped me realize that it's okay to make mistakes and accept that it's one of the ways you really learn a lesson.

Success Lesson #5:
Good choices and hard work are a potent combination.

- ## What are you most proud of in your career?
  Construction Manager: I have great hopes and great dreams and I fully intend to make them happen for myself. I don't have anything more than anyone else. I was not given some golden opportunity or cut any breaks. I simply chose a different path than most people my age.

  Equipment Manager: I was president of the Association of Equipment Managers and Professionals, an education-based organization. I had 15 board members to direct and 800 national members to please in order to make sure that this organization was the leader in the industry.

  Electrician: I was able to be the mechanical, electrical, and plumbing coordinator on a $50 million dollar project that took two years to complete. I now drive by the building on a regular basis and know I helped "build" it.

  CEO: Becoming the first woman president of the American Society of Civil Engineers in its 152-year history. The organization has over 133,000 members.

  Career Education Director: Building new programs such as those that bring students from all over the country to our legislative conference in Washington, D.C., and then seeing them learn from and enjoy that experience. I also enjoy "raising the bar" for existing programs like raising more funds so we can offer bigger prizes in our competition.

  Marketing Manager: Last year I was responsible for bringing leads that led to more than $20 million worth of "real" projects. As a result I won the National Association of Women in Construction Rookie of the Year Award last year and I've been nominated for their Member of the Year Award this year.

  Mechanical Engineer: So far, my proudest accomplishment has been to have built a solid reputation as someone who my clients can trust to always exceed their expectations. Without this, I don't think I would be as far along as I am today.

Architect: Writing my master's thesis on a subject that really meant something to me, and then being able to apply that knowledge to my work.

Success Lesson #6:
You can learn from other people's mistakes.

- **Is there anything you wish you had done differently?**

    Equipment Manager: Looking back, I think I did great for myself and my family. Being happy and healthy is the best part.

    Electrician: I wish I had started earlier, so that I could retire sooner.

    Career Education Director: There is very little I would change. Maybe take more marketing classes earlier in life.

    Marketing Manager: Sometimes I wish that I had taken out college loans so I could be more involved in art. But mostly I'm glad I get to use my earnings for me and don't have to pay back any student loans. Fortunately, I enjoy what I do. I make the job my own. Someone else may not be as creative in it.

    Mechanical Engineer: No, I don't have any regrets about what I have done. That's not to say I didn't make any mistakes, but that experience is what helps us learn and grow and that's what evolution is all about.

    Architect: I probably would have benefited from taking time off between high school and university.

Success Lesson #7:
A little advice goes a long way.

- **What advice do you have for a young person just getting started?**

    Construction Manager: My job is dangerous. Often times I am the only female physically present on the jobsite. Each and every day is an experience and a lesson in life and in construction. But I learned from something Helen Keller once said, "Character cannot be developed in ease and quiet. Only through experience of trial and suffering can the soul be strengthened, ambition inspired, and success achieved."

Electrician: The union apprenticeships offer an education while earning a living. The only other place like that is the military, which pays for your education after you have worked. An apprenticeship allows the two to overlap and then if you decide to pursue higher education, you have a job to pay for it, and a skill no one can take away from you.

Equipment Manager: Work hard and get the best education you can get or afford. This is a great career even starting at ground level as a mechanic. Do not be afraid of a little dirt: some of the best-paying jobs in the industry may require getting dirty.

CEO: Goal setting. Goals need to be set and reviewed each year for 12 months, five years, and 10 years. Your activities should be centered around your goals which are the things you want to accomplish and get out of both your career and life. Also, it is important to get a master's degree and to have lifelong learning to continue to be on the cutting edge.

Career Education Director: Try as many different things as you can. Don't worry too much about finding your niche or specialty. That will come in time. You may have talents you never even realized. Don't be afraid to try the things that scare you, like public speaking. Keep your mind open to new and different opinions.

Marketing Manager: Work hard. I am the first person at Kajima to fill the business development role without a degree in construction. It can be done.

Mechanical Engineer: My advice is to always be aware of what is happening in the world around you, create a plan that gives you a sense of direction, constantly reassess what you are doing and whether it makes you happy, and to take action!

Life is too short and work is too big a part of who we are for us to be unsatisfied with doing it.

Architect: Work in an architect's office or in a construction company during a summer break if possible.

Big Activity #7:
who knows what you need to know?

It's one thing to read about conducting an informational interview, but it's another thing altogether to actually do one. Now it's your turn to shine. Just follow these steps for doing it like a pro!

Step 1: Identify the people you want to talk to about their work.

Step 2: Set up a convenient time to meet either in person or to talk over the phone.

Step 3: Make up a list of questions that reflect things you'd really like to know about that person's work. Go for the open questions you just read about.

Step 4: Talk away! Take notes as your interviewee responds to each question.

Step 5: Use your notes to write up a "news" article that describes the person and his or her work.

Step 6: Place all your notes and the finished "news" article in your Big Question AnswerBook.

Big Activity #7: **who knows what you need to know?**

contact information	appointments/sample questions
name company title address phone email	day time location sample questions:
name company title address phone email	day time location sample questions:
name company title address phone email	day time location sample questions:

CONTACT INFO

Big Activity #7: **who knows what you need to know?**

questions	answers

INTERVIEW NOTES

Big Activity #7: **who knows what you need to know?**

questions	answers

INTERVIEW NOTES

Big Activity #7: **who knows what you need to know?**

NEWS

Big Activity #7: **who knows what you need to know?**

NEWS

Big Question #8:
how can you find out what a career is really like?

There are some things you just have to figure out for yourself. Things like whether your interest in pursuing a career in marine biology is practical if you plan to live near the Mojave Desert.

Other things you have to see for yourself. Words are sometimes not enough when it comes to conveying what a job is really like on a day-to-day basis—what it looks like, sounds like, and feels like.

Here are a few ideas for conducting an on-the-job reality check.

identify typical types of workplaces

Think of all the places that jobs like the ones you like take place. Almost all of the careers in this book, or ones very similar to them, exist in the corporate world, in the public sector, and in the military. And don't forget the option of going into business for yourself!

For example: Are you interested in public relations? You can find a place for yourself in almost any sector of our economy. Of course, companies definitely want to promote their products. But don't limit yourself to the Fortune 500 corporate world. Hospitals, schools, and manufacturers need your services. Cities, states, and even countries also need your services. They want to increase tourism, get businesses to relocate there, and convince workers to live there or students to study there. Each military branch needs to recruit new members and to show how they are using the money they receive from the government for medical research, taking care of families, and other non-news-breaking uses. Charities, community organizations, and even religious groups want to promote the good things they are doing so that they will get more members, volunteers, contributions, and funding. Political candidates, parties, and special interest groups all want to promote their messages. Even actors, dancers, and writers need to promote themselves.

Not interested in public relations but know you want a career that involves lots of writing? You've thought about becoming the more obvious choices—novelist, newspaper reporter, or English teacher. But you don't want to overlook other interesting possibilities, do you?

What if you also enjoy technical challenges? Someone has to write the documentation for all those computer games and software.

Love cars? Someone has to write those owner's manuals too.

Ditto on those government reports about safety and environmental standards for industries.

Maybe community service is your thing. You can mix your love for helping people with writing grant proposals seeking funds for programs at hospitals, day care centers, or rehab centers.

Talented in art and design? Those graphics you see in magazine advertisements, on your shampoo bottle, and on a box of cereal all have to be created by someone.

That someone could be you.

find out about the job outlook

Organizations like the U.S. Bureau of Labor Statistics spend a lot of time and energy gathering data on what kinds of jobs are most in demand now and what kinds are projected to be in demand in the future. Find out what the job outlook is for a career you like. A good resource for this data can be found on-line at America's Career InfoNet at *www.acinet.org/acinet.*

This information will help you understand whether the career options you find most appealing are viable. In other words, job outlook data will give you a better sense of your chances of actually finding gainful employment in your chosen profession—a rather important consideration from any standpoint.

Be realistic. You may really, really want to be a film critic at a major newspaper. Maybe your ambition is to become the next Roger Ebert.

Think about this. How many major newspapers are there? Is it reasonable to pin all your career hopes on a job for which there are only about 10 positions in the whole country? That doesn't mean that it's impossible to achieve your ambition. After all, someone has to fill those positions. It should just temper your plans with realism and perhaps encourage you to have a back-up plan, just in case.

look at training requirements

Understand what it takes to prepare yourself for a specific job. Some jobs require only a high school diploma. Others require a couple of years of technical training, while still others require four years or more in college.

Be sure to investigate a variety of training options. Look at training programs and colleges you may like to attend. Check out their websites to see what courses are required for the major you want. Make sure you're willing to "do the time" in school to prepare yourself for a particular occupation.

see for yourself

There's nothing quite like seeing for yourself what a job is like. Talk with a teacher or guidance counselor to arrange a job-shadowing opportunity with someone who is in the job or in a similar one.

Job shadowing is an activity that involves actually spending time at work with someone to see what a particular job is like up close and personal. It's an increasingly popular option and your school may participate in specially designated job-shadowing days. For some especially informative resources on job shadowing, visit *www.jobshadow.org*.

Another way to test-drive different careers is to find summer jobs and internships that are similar to the career you hope to pursue.

make a Plan B

Think of the alternatives! Often it's not possible to have a full-time job in the field you love. Some jobs just don't pay enough to meet the needs of every person or family. Maybe you recognize that you don't have the talent, drive, or commitment to rise to the top. Or, perhaps you can't afford the years of work it takes to get established or you place a higher priority on spending time with family than that career might allow.

If you can see yourself in any of those categories, DO NOT GIVE UP on what you love! There is always more than one way to live out your dreams. Look at some of the other possibilities in this book. Find a way to integrate your passion into other jobs or your free time.

Lots of people manage to accomplish this in some fairly impressive ways. For instance, the Knicks City Dancers, known for their incredible performances and for pumping up the crowd at Knicks basketball games, include an environmental engineer, a TV news assignment editor, and a premed student, in addition to professional dancers. The Broadband Pickers, a North Texas bluegrass band, is made up of five lawyers and one businessman. In fact, even people who are extremely successful in a field that they love find ways to indulge their other passions. Paul Newman, the actor and director, not only drives race cars as a hobby, but also produces a line of gourmet foods and donates the profits to charity.

Get the picture? Good. Hang in there and keep moving forward in your quest to find your way toward a great future.

Big Activity #8:
how can you find out what a career is really like?

This activity will help you conduct a reality check about your future career in two ways. First, it prompts you to find out more about the nitty-gritty details you really need to know to make a well-informed career choice. Second, it helps you identify strategies for getting a firsthand look at what it's like to work in a given profession—day in and day out.

Here's how to get started:

Step 1: Write the name of the career you're considering at the top of a sheet of paper (or use the following worksheets if this is your book).

Step 2: Create a checklist (or, if this is your book, use the one provided on the following pages) covering two types of reality-check items.

First, list four types of information to investigate:
- training requirements
- typical workplaces
- job outlook
- similar occupations

Second, list three types of opportunities to pursue:
- job shadowing
- apprenticeship
- internship

Step 3: Use resources such as America's Career InfoNet at **www.acinet. org** and Career OneStop at **www.careeronestop.org** to seek out the information you need.

Step 4: Make an appointment with your school guidance counselor to discuss how to pursue hands-on opportunities to learn more about this occupation. Use the space provided on the following worksheets to jot down preliminary contact information and a brief summary of why or why not each career is right for you.

Step 5: When you're finished, place these notes in your Big Question AnswerBook.

Big Activity #8: **how can you find out
what a career is really like?**

career choice:	
training requirements	
typical workplaces	
job outlook	
similar occupations	

INFORMATION

Big Activity #8: **how can you find out
what a career is really like?**

job shadowing	when: where: who: observations and impressions:
apprenticeship	when: where: who: observations and impressions:
internship	when: where: who: observations and impressions:

OPPORTUNITIES

Big Question #9:
how do you know when you've made the right choice?

When it comes right down to it, finding the career that's right for you is like shopping in a mall with 12,000 different stores. Finding the right fit may require trying on lots of different options.

All the Big Questions you've answered so far have been designed to expand your career horizons and help you clarify what you really want in a career. The next step is to see how well you've managed to integrate your interests, capabilities, goals, and ambitions with the realities of specific opportunities.

There are two things for you to keep in mind as you do this.

First, recognize the value of all the hard work you did to get to this point. If you've already completed the first eight activities thoughtfully and honestly, whatever choices you make will be based on solid knowledge about yourself and your options. You've learned to use a process that works just as well now, when you're trying to get an inkling of what you want to do with your life, as it will later when you have solid job offers on the table and need to make decisions that will affect your life and family.

Second, always remember that sometimes, even when you do everything right, things don't turn out the way you'd planned. That's called life. It happens. And it's not the end of the world. Even if you make what seems to be a bad choice, know this— there's no such thing as a wasted experience. The paths you take, the training you receive, the people you meet—they ultimately fall together like puzzle pieces to make you who you are and prepare you for what you're meant to do.

That said, here's a strategy to help you confirm that you are making the very best choices you can.

Big Activity #9:
how do you know when you've made the right choice?

One way to confirm that the choices you are making are right for you is to look at both sides of this proverbial coin: what you are looking for and what each career offers. The following activity will help you think this through.

Step 1: To get started, make two charts with four columns (or, if this is your book, use the following worksheet).

Step 2: Label the first column of the first chart as "Yes Please!" Under this heading list all the qualities you absolutely must have in a future job. This might include factors such as the kind of training you'd prefer to pursue (college, apprenticeship, etc.); the type of place where you'd like to work (big office, high-tech lab, in the great outdoors, etc.); and the sorts of people you want to work with (children, adults, people with certain needs, etc.). It may also include salary requirements or dress code preferences.

Step 3: Now at the top of the next three columns write the names of three careers you are considering. (This is a little like Big Activity #3 where you examined your work values. But now you know a lot more and you're ready to zero in on specific careers.)

Step 4: Go down the list and use an X to indicate careers that do indeed feature the desired preferences. Use an O to indicate those that do not.

Step 5: Tally up the number of Xs and Os at the bottom of each career column to find out which comes closest to your ideal job.

Step 6: In the first column of the second chart add a heading called "No Thanks!" This is where you'll record the factors you simply prefer not to deal with. Maybe long hours, physically demanding work, or jobs that require years of advanced training just don't cut it for you. Remember that part of figuring out what you do want to do involves understanding what you don't want to do.

Step 7: Repeat steps 2 through 5 for these avoid-at-all-costs preferences as you did for the must-have preferences above.

Big Activity #9: **how do you know when you've made the right choice?**

yes please!	career #1	career #2	career #3
totals	__X__O	__X__O	__X__O

Big Activity #9: **how do you know when you've made the right choice?**

no thanks!	career #1	career #2	career #3
totals	__X__O	__X__O	__X__O

Big Question #10:
what's next?

Think of this experience as time well invested in your future. And expect it to pay off in a big way down the road. By now, you have worked (and perhaps wrestled) your way through nine important questions:

- ❓ Big Question #1: **who are you?**
- ❓ Big Question #2: **what are your interests and strengths?**
- ❓ Big Question #3: **what are your work values?**
- ❓ Big Question #4: **what is your work personality?**
- ❓ Big Question #5: **do you have the right skills?**
- ❓ Big Question #6: **are you on the right path?**
- ❓ Big Question #7: **who knows what you need to know?**
- ❓ Big Question #8: **how can you find out what a career is really like?**
- ❓ Big Question #9: **how do you know when you've made the right choice?**

But what if you still don't have a clue about what you want to do with your life?

Don't worry. You're talking about one of the biggest life decisions you'll ever make. These things take time.

It's okay if you don't have all the definitive answers yet. At least you do know how to go about finding them. The process you've used to work through this book is one that you can rely on throughout your life to help you sort through the options and make sound career decisions.

So what's next?

More discoveries, more exploration, and more experimenting with success are what come next. Keep at it and you're sure to find your way to wherever your dreams and ambitions lead you.

And, just for good measure, here's one more Big Activity to help point you in the right direction.

Big Activity #10:
what's next?

List five things you can do to move forward in your career planning process (use a separate sheet if you need to). Your list may include tasks such as talking to your guidance counselor about resources your school makes available, checking out colleges or other types of training programs that can prepare you for your life's work, or finding out about job-shadowing or internship opportunities in your community. Remember to include any appropriate suggestions from the Get Started Now! list included with each career profile in Section 2 of this book.

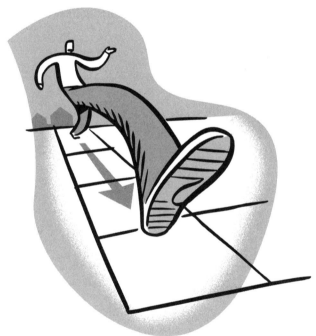

Big Activity #10: **what's next?**

career planning to-do list

1

2

3

4

5

a final word

You are now officially equipped with the tools you need to track down a personally appropriate profession any time you have the need or desire. You've discovered more about who you are and what you want. You've explored a variety of career options within a very important industry. You've even taken it upon yourself to experiment with what it might be like to actually work in certain occupations.

Now it's up to you to put all this newfound knowledge to work for you. While you're at it, here's one more thing to keep in mind: Always remember that there's no such thing as a wasted experience. Certainly some experiences are more positive than others, but they all teach us something.

Chances are you may not get everything right the first time out. It may turn out that you were incorrect about how much you would love to go to a certain college or pursue a particular profession. That doesn't mean you're doomed to failure. It simply means that you've lived and learned. Sometimes you just won't know for sure about one direction or another until you try things out a bit. Nothing about your future has to be written in stone. Allow yourself some freedom to experiment with various options until you find something that really clicks for you.

Figuring out what you want to do with the rest of your life is a big deal. It's probably one of the most exciting and among the most intimidating decisions you'll ever make. It's a decision that warrants clearheaded thought and wholehearted investigation. It's a process that's likely to take you places you never dared imagine if you open yourself up to all the possibilities. Take a chance on yourself and seek out and follow your most valued hopes and dreams into the workplace.

Best wishes for a bright future!

Appendix

a virtual support team

As you continue your quest to determine just what it is you want to do with your life, you'll find that you are not alone. There are many people and organizations who want to help you succeed. Here are two words of advice—let them! Take advantage of all the wonderful resources so readily available to you.

The first place to start is your school's guidance center. There you are quite likely to find a variety of free resources which include information about careers, colleges, and other types of training opportunities; details about interesting events, job shadowing activities, and internship options; and access to useful career assessment tools.

In addition, since you are the very first generation on the face of the earth to have access to a world of information just the click of a mouse away—use it! The following Internet resources provide all kinds of information and ideas that can help you find your future.

make an informed choice

Following are five of the very best career-oriented websites currently on-line. Be sure to bookmark these websites and visit them often as you consider various career options.

America's Career Info Net *www.acinet.org/acinet/default.asp*

Quite possibly the most comprehensive source of career exploration anywhere, this U.S. Department of Labor website includes all kinds of current information about wages, market conditions, employers, and employment trends. Make sure to visit the site's career video library where you'll find links to over 450 videos featuring real people doing real jobs.

Careers & Colleges *www.careersandcolleges.com*

Each year Careers & Colleges publishes four editions of *Careers & Colleges* magazine, designed to help high school students set and meet their academic, career, and financial goals. Ask your guidance counselor about receiving free copies. You'll also want to visit the excellent Careers and Colleges website. Here you'll encounter their "Virtual Guidance Counselor," an interactive career database that allows you to match your interests with college majors or careers that are right for you.

Career Voyages *www.careervoyages.gov*

This website is brought to you compliments of collaboration between the U.S. Department of Labor and the U.S. Department of Education and is designed especially for students like you. Here you'll find information on high-growth, high-demand occupations and the skills and education needed to attain those jobs.

Job Shadow *www.jobshadow.org*

See your future via a variety of on-line virtual job-shadowing videos and interviews featuring people with fascinating jobs.

My Cool Career *www.mycoolcareer.com*

This website touts itself as the "coolest career dream site for teens and 20's." See for yourself as you work your way through a variety of useful self-assessment quizzes, listen to an assortment of on-line career shows, and explore all kinds of career resources.

investigate local opportunities

To get a better understanding of employment happenings in your state, visit these state-specific career information websites.

Alabama
www.ajb.org/al
www.al.plusjobs.com

Alaska
www.jobs.state.ak.us
www.akcis.org/default.htm

Arizona
www.ajb.org/az
www.ade.state.az.us/cte/AZCrn project10.asp

Arkansas
www.ajb.org/ar
www.careerwatch.org
www.ioscar.org/ar

California
www.calmis.ca.gov
www.ajb.org/ca
www.eurekanet.org

Colorado
www.coloradocareer.net
www.coworkforce.com/lmi

Connecticut
www1.ctdol.state.ct.us/jcc
www.ctdol.state.ct.us/lmi

Delaware
www.ajb.org/de
www.delewareworks.com

District of Columbia
www.ajb.org/dc
www.dcnetworks.org

Florida
www.Florida.access.bridges.com
www.employflorida.net

Georgia
www.gcic.peachnet.edu
  (Ask your school guidance counselor for your school's free password and access code)
www.dol.state.ga.us/js

Hawaii
www.ajb.org/hi
www.careerkokua.org

Idaho
www.ajb.org/id
www.cis.idaho.gov

Illinois
www.ajb.org/il
www.ilworkinfo.com

Indiana
www.ajb.org/in
http://icpac.indiana.edu

Iowa
www.ajb.org/ia
www.state.ia.us/iccor

Kansas
www.ajb.org/ks
www.kansasjoblink.com/ada

Kentucky
www.ajb.org/ky

Louisiana
www.ajb.org/la
www.ldol.state.la.us/jobpage.asp

Maine
www.ajb.org/me
www.maine.gov/labor/lmis

Maryland
www.ajb.org/md
www.careernet.state.md.us

Massachusetts
www.ajb.org/ma
http://masscis.intocareers.org

Michigan
www.mois.org

Minnesota
www.ajb.org/mn
www.iseek.org

Mississippi
www.ajb.org/ms
www.mscareernet.org

Missouri
www.ajb.org/mo
www.greathires.org

Montana
www.ajb.org/mt
http://jsd.dli.state.mt.us/mjshome.asp

Nebraska
www.ajb.org/ne
www.careerlink.org

New Hampshire
www.nhes.state.nh.us

New Jersey
www.ajb.org/nj
www.wnjpin.net/coei

New Mexico
www.ajb.org/nm
www.dol.state.nm.us/soicc/upto21.html

Nevada
www.ajb.org/nv
http://nvcis.intocareers.org

New York
www.ajb.org/ny
www.nycareerzone.org

North Carolina
www.ajb.org/nc
www.ncsoicc.org
www.nccareers.org

North Dakota
www.ajb.org/nd
www.imaginend.com
www.ndcrn.com/students

Ohio
www.ajb.org/oh
https://scoti.ohio.gov/scoti_lexs

Oklahoma
www.ajb.org/ok
www.okcareertech.org/guidance
http://okcrn.org

Oregon
www.hsd.k12.or.us/crls

Pennsylvania
www.ajb.org/pa
www.pacareerlink.state.pa.us

Rhode Island
www.ajb.org/ri
www.dlt.ri.gov/lmi/jobseeker.htm

South Carolina
www.ajb.org/sc
www.scois.org/students.htm

South Dakota
www.ajb.org/sd

Tennessee
www.ajb.org/tn
www.tcids.utk.edu

Texas
www.ajb.org/tx
www.ioscar.org/tx
www.cdr.state.tx.us/Hotline/Hotline.html

Utah
www.ajb.org/ut
http://jobs.utah.gov/wi/occi.asp

Vermont
www.ajb.org/vt
www.vermontjoblink.com
www.vtlmi.info/oic.cfm

Virginia
www.ajb.org/va
www.vacrn.net

Washington
www.ajb.org/wa
www.workforceexplorer.com
www.wa.gov/esd/lmea/soicc/sohome.htm

West Virginia
www.ajb.org/wv
www.state.wv.us/bep/lmi

Wisconsin
www.ajb.org/wi
www.careers4wi.wisc.edu
http://wiscareers.wisc.edu/splash.asp

Wyoming
www.ajb.org/wy
http://uwadmnweb.uwyo.edu/SEO/wcis.htm

get a job

Whether you're curious about the kinds of jobs currently in big demand or you're actually looking for a job, the following websites are a great place to do some virtual job-hunting.

America's Job Bank *www.ajb.org*

Another example of your (or, more accurately, your parent's) tax dollars at work, this well-organized website is sponsored by the U.S. Department of Labor. Job seekers can post resumes and use the site's search engines to search through over a million job listings by location or by job type.

Monster.com *www.monster.com*

One of the Internet's most widely used employment websites, this is where you can search for specific types of jobs in specific parts of the country, network with millions of people, and find useful career advice.

explore by special interests

An especially effective way to explore career options is to look at careers associated with a personal interest or fascination with a certain type of industry. The following websites help you narrow down your options in a focused way.

What Interests You? *www.bls.gov/k12*

This Bureau of Labor Statistics website provides information about careers associated with 12 special interest areas: math, reading, science, social studies, music and arts, building and fixing things, helping people, computers, law, managing money, sports, and nature.

Construct My Future *www.constructmyfuture.com*

With over $600 billion annually devoted to new construction projects, about 6 million Americans build careers in this industry. This website, sponsored by the Association of Equipment Distributors, the Association of Equipment Manufacturers, and Associated General Contractors, introduces an interesting array of construction-related professions.

Dream It Do It *www.dreamit-doit.com*

In order to make manufacturing a preferred career choice by 2010, the National Association of Manufacturing's Center for Workforce Success is reaching out to young adults and, their parents, educators, communities, and policy-makers to change their minds about manufacturing's future and its careers. This website introduces high-demand 21st-century manufacturing professions many will find surprising and worthy of serious consideration.

Get Tech *www.gettech.org*

Another award-winning website from the National Association of Manufacturing.

Take Another Look *www.Nrf.com/content/foundation/rcp/main.htm*

The National Retail Federation challenges students to take another look at their industry by introducing a wide variety of careers associated with marketing and advertising, store management, sales, distribution and logistics, e-commerce, and more.

Index

Page numbers in **boldface** indicate main articles. Page numbers in *italics* indicate photographs.